# MONUMENTS:
# A VISION OF HARMONY

# MONUMENTS:
# A VISION OF HARMONY

**Dr. A.P. Singh**

AGAM KALA PRAKASHAN
DELHI - 110 052

First Published 2010



ISBN : 978-81-7320-093-9



*Published by:*
Dr. Agam Prasad, M.A., Ph.D., Diploma in Museology
For **Agam Kala Prakashan**
34, Central Market, Ashok Vihar
Delhi - 110 052
Tel.: 27212195, 47098 550, 65688806-7
Fax: 91-11-27212195
Email: agambooks@gmail.com, agambook@yahoo.com

*Composed by:*
Aman Printographics
Delhi - 110 052
Mobile: 9891395309

*Printed by:*
Salasar Imaging Systems
Delhi-110 035

Printed in India

***Dedicated to Mahakaleshwar***

# CONTENTS

# PREFACE

India is the cosmopolitan centres of different religion. The ancient and eternal spirit sprang up here with a perfect amalgam of abundance continuity and excellence in ever thousands monuments from prehistoric period to Mughal, Maratha period. These monuments are located from North to South and East to West, providing us a coherent picture of open air museum of monuments, a vision of Hormony.

A comprehensive scientific recording of the monument and other cultural heritage have been assessed and subjected to our critical study.

In the preparation of this monograph, many hands have offered invaluable contribution, and it will be unfare on my part to remain silent about those who have contributed in giving a shape of a book.

Shri Shiv Pal Singh my eldest son carried out the photography of the monuments and the layout was prepared by Dr. Harpal Singh my younger son.

I am extremely thankful to Dr. Rahman Ali Retd. Prof. in Ancient Indian History & Culture and Archaeology, Vikram University Ujjain, who was always very helpful to me in preparation of this book.

It is beyond expression to account for the encouragement given to, my wife Smt. Meena Devi and daughter in laws Smt. Priya Lata and Dr. Puja Singh due to which I could undertake this work in spite of preoccupations with family.

Apart from the above mentioned scholars and well wishers, record my sincere gratitude to all those whose names are not mentioned but helped me in various ways to complete this monograph.

Mr. Pankaj Gajbhiye, Annapurna Enterprizes has typed the manuscript neatly inspite of his preoccupation. I thank him for his sincere help.

I am also thankful to Dr. Agam Prasad and Staff of Agam Kala Prakashan for publishing this monograph in such a short time.

**Dr. A.P. Singh**
Bhopal, Mahashiva Ratri,
Phalgunkrishna-14
V.S. 2065-66

# LIST OF ILLUSTRATIONS

**Figures**



**Plates**

Chapter 1

# GEOGRAPHICAL EXPANSE

The vast geographical expanse of India is surrounded and bounded by the great lofty Himalayas on its west side is Arabian sea and likewise the Bay of Bengal is in the east, south side is touched by Indian ocean. It is interesting to note that rhomboidal peninsulas shores are splashed in three sides by those oceans. Infact the peninsula is a piece of land that is sussocended by oceans on three sides.

The total area of India posses about 3.28 million square kilometers.

The north-south extent from Kashmir to Kanyakumari is about 3200 km. Likewise the distance between Arunachal Pradesh to Kuchchh is 2900 km.

The lofty Himalayan mountains, The great Indian desert, the northern plains, the uneven plateaee surface and the coasts and islands present a diversity of land forms.

There is a great variety in the climate, vegetation, wild life as well as in the language and culture.

The north-west, south-east lying Himalayan ranges have given Indian tesetory a certain seclusion from outside influences- both political and cultural as well as climate;

It is true fact that these ranges have been penetrated in India's past history particularly this has been so in the north west where not only the two famous routes. Viz, the Khyber and the Bolan passes have a every access to and from Afghanistan and Baluchistan. Apart from the above routes the Gomal pass was also used extensively by the invaders and refugee, traders and travellers from central and western Asia.

Thus the Indian seclusion have been violated. Thus the foreigners come in and they have spread into the Indo gangetic plains and beyond by the most suitable lines of communications.

India is, however approachable by sea from the west and south and south- east as well by the difficult, hilly and thickly forested country on the north east.

The west has been the major gateway during the historical times even during historic period and proto historic times as well.

In preceding pages we have discussed about the diversity of physical features such as mountains, plateaus, plains, coasts and Ilands, standing as sentinels in north are the Lofty snow capped Himalayas. The Himalayan mountains are divided into three main parallel ranges. The northern most is the great Himalaya or Himadri.[1] The world's highest peaks are located in this range. Middle Himalaya or Himachal lies to the south of Himadri. Many popular hill stations are situated here. The third is the Shivalik range situated in the southern most ranges.

The north Indian plains lie to the south of the Himalayas. They are gradually level and flat. These are formed by the alluvial deposits laid down by the rivers the Indus, the Ganga, Brahmaputra and their tributaries. These river plain provide fertile land for cultivation. That is why these plains are thickly populated.

---

[1] See map of India showing mountain/hills ranges.

In the western part of India lies the great Indian desert. It is a dry, hot and sandy stretch of land. It has very little vegetation. only thorny bushes can survive here.

To, the south of northern plains lies the peninsular plateau. It is triangular in shape. The relief is highly uneven. This is a region with numerous hill ranges and valleys. Aravali hills, one of the oldest ranges of the world, boarder it on the north-west side.

The Vindhayas and Satpuras are the important ranges of Madhya Pradesh.

The river Narmada and Tapti flow through these ranges. These are the west flowing rivers that drain into the Arabian sea.

The western ghat or Sahyadris border the plateau in the west and eastern ghats provide the eastern boundary. While the western ghats are almost continuous, the eastern ghats are broken and uneven. The plateau is rich in minerals like coal and iron.

To the west of the western ghats and the east of the eastern ghats lie the coastal plain.

The western coastal plains are very narrow. The eastern coastal plains are much broader there are a number of east flowing rivers. The rivers Mahanadi, Godavari, Krishna and Kaveri drain into the Bay of Bengal. These rivers have formed fertile deltas at their mouth.

The Sunderban delta is formed, where Ganga and Brahmaputtra flow into the Bay of Bengal. The entire land of central India a natures pradise endowed with extensive forest resources, rich and fertile soil, perennial rivers, varied and wide flora and fauna and vast expense of cultivable area, has been a meeting ground of different cultures since the earliest times. Two stone age industries of the north and peninsular India are available here. It has the largest group of prehistoric rock painted rock shelter (Bhimbetka), noted World Heritage Monument and it is here (Besanagar -Vidisha) that the contemporaneity of the chalcolithic and painted grey ware cultures has been noticed for the first time.

Many aspects of Indian art and architecture appear to have originated and flourished in this past of the country. The earliest temple (4th-3rd Century B.C.) in its fully developed form Besanagar elliptical temple, is an example of this, Apart from this number of temples of Gupta period in various stages of tits developments have also been found in Madhya Pradesh.

Udaigir cave temple, Sanchi, Tigowa, Bhumra, Nachra is significant examples. Likewise elaborately carved and elegantly spired temples of the Aryan style viz Khajuraho, Udaipur, Un, Bhoram-deo.

It is interesting to point out here that a temple situated in Gwalior fort possesses a composite architectural feature of Aryan and Dravidian a notable contributions of this state.

Being located in central part of India, Madhya Pradesh region, from the strategic position has all the varieties of fort, including the largest fort of the world Mandu Fort[1] and most impregnable and invincible forts like Gwalior, Raisen, Ashirgarh.

Many large sized yakasha sculptures of Mauryan and Sunga periods in Madhya Pradesh are the unique archaeological remains of this region than in other states of India.

The indiginious art of Bharhut and Sanchi containing symbolic representation embellished with cosmic expressions and representing the specimen of the Buddhist art in India.

Likewise the symbolic representation of Ganga and Yamuna in Iconic forms and maiden depictions of puranic themes are good examples of Madhya Pradesh region.

[1] Dr. Singh A.P., Forts of India Vol - I and II, P-70, 130.

It is interesting to mention over here that the entire land of this province is most suitable and feasible for construction of monuments since the earliest times of later periods from the defensive point of view.

The whole land of this province is devided by chain of hill series, Vez, Vindhyan range (The impregnable range), Bhander and Kaimur ranges situated in west and easterly direction.

It is because of the above topography of the land the various dynasties of ancient India were fascinated to construct the defensive forts, palaces and temples mosques at their appropriate time and positions.

Geologically the traps of upper part are noteworthy because of their unique geological phenomenon i.e. Horst in nature obviously, it inspired the constructions of impregnable forts here. A large number of fort were constructed in Madhya Pradesh rather than any other states of India.

Likewise other monuments, from prehistoric times to modern period are the main feature of this central India region. Looking to the above mentioned factors, responsible for suitability of raising monuments in Madhya Pradesh, Special mention regarding Geography and topography is essential, need a special mention over here.

Safar as the defensive part of the region is concerned, the fort in lower postion, however, cannot be overlooked because by nature they are covered by dense forest and are situated on unapproachable top surface of the hills.

Obviously another aspect of protection, hence so many forts were raised in this part at the unique strategic point. The forts like Asirgarh, Ajaigarh, Kalanjar remind us their past glory in the history of India.

After crossing river Tapti towards south the Island type of plateau sarts.

Geologically, the rocks formation of the region consists of Vindhyan ranges and granite-gneiss. The high ridges situated in south and south eastern directions annexed with Bhander and Kaimur ranges are inaccessible. This geologically Madhya Pradesh may be divided into following major parts.

High and low plateaus annexed with plains of the river sides. The maximum height among the hill ranges of Madhya Pradesh is the Satpura range which is 1350 meters above mean sea level, next to it comes the plateaus of Bahelkhand in which the highest range measures 1130 metres.

The lowest ranges are of 200 metres in the Mahadeo valley while the Narmada and Chambal valleys are of 150 metres in height.

The belt falling in south of Narmada-Son axis is known as Satpura range which is formed by granite gneiss, Gondwana system and Deccan-trap, the eastern part of which is called Maikal range which is serrated in ridges and covered by thick forests.

A part from the two plateaus mentioned above another plateau in the east, the northern part of which is known as Baghelkhand, the plain central part is called Chhattisgarh, is segmented to Dandakaranya thickly forested patch of the land. The plains of Chhattisgarh are formed of erroded rocks matter of Kudapah rock belts. The pre-cambrian granite and Dharwar rock are again found in the land of Dandakaranya - land of low and high altitude plateus and valleys.

Besides the unique geological wealth it is in fact a water shed for hundreds of rivers that flow out of the state in all directions feeding Ganges and the Yamuna to the north, the Narmada and Tapti flowing westward to the Arabian sea, and the Wardha, Wainganga and Mahanadi flowing north and east directions towards the Bay of Bengal.

The state lies mainly on the table land of central India. To the north it is bounded by the Upper Gangetic valley. The plateaus continues into the state of Andhra Pradesh to the south and Orissa to the east. The arid tract of Rajasthan lies to the west.

The latitude 19°-26° N. indicate a tropical climate of the region. As regards the season in the north India there is hot dry summer during the months of April-June generally followed by monsoon during the July-September months and a cool and relatively dry winter season which have played important roles for the favourable seasons for invasions.

The area is divided by the ranges of low mountain intersected by river valleys, which breaks up the state into different regions. The main valleys of Narmada and Son run diagonally across the state. Both rivers rise close together in the Maikal ranges The Narmada flowing west by south between the Vindhya and Satpura ranges creating a fertile zone between the hills, while the Son does the same as it flows north- towards Ganges.

The Vindhya and other ranges to the north are in falling gradient and finally merge with the Gangetic plain.

The southern hills are generally higher and spread over a large area running down with some breaks in the Andhra Pradesh. The high lands of son and Maikal which form the eastern shoulder of these hills descend into the Chhattisgarh plains - extending over the districts of Raigarh, Bilaspur, Raipur, Durg, Rajnandgaon and northern part of Baster. South of these plains is another range of low hills, forming the plain area.

The peculiar features of earth in peninsula India is segment of the most ancient complex of rock beds that stand upon a firm and immovable foundation that have, for an immense number of ages, remained so impressive amid all the revolutions that have again and again changed the face of the earth. Such phenomenon of the earth construction have facilitated the builders to raise the fort on the surface providing strength to the fortification walls. It is noteworthy that the "HORST" type of crusts segments had remained a stable land mass of great frigidity and has been unceffected by any folding movement. The forts like Gwalior, Asirgarh[1], Lafagarh, Raisen are a few examples constructed over such "HORST".

Vindhya mountains : Satpura range - The rocky contry whch rises gradually from the south of the Gangetic plains culminates in the a highlands of central India- Indore, Bhopal, Bundelkhand region are situated in this region. The Vindhyas are for their greater part composed of horizontally bedded sedimentary rocks. South of the Vindhyas, and roughly parallel with their direction, are the Satpura Mountains. The chain of ridges commences from Gaya and Rewa, runs south of Narmada valley and north of Tapti valley, and stretches westward through the Rajpipla hills to the western ghat. The Vindhya and the Satpura chain form together the back-bone of middle India. Very large parts of the Satpura, both in the west and the east, are formed of bedded basalts; The central part has a core of granitoid and metamorphic rocks, overlain by Gondwana sand stone. Parts of the Satpura give proof of having been folded and upheaved.

In preceding pages we have discussed the geographical set up as wel as the nature of the rock formations and hill-rages in different areas of Madhya Pradesh. The directions of the rivers flow and the climate have also been taken into consideration and now it is essential to discuss the main geographical factors which were responsible for selection of the spot for building forts and fortifications in different periods of history of India in general and Madhya Pradesh in particular.

The minute observations and scientific survey of the Forts and Fortifications reveal that certain regions attracted the builders to select the particular spot for raising such monuments. Three factors may be discussed as follows:

First of all, we may, however, consider the composition of rock- beds upon which the foundation of the forts are layed. Geologically, the surface of rocks where these forts were raised are sedimentary rocks which possess a peculiar feature in its formation, i.e., they are horizontally bedded. This particular feature is very useful for supporting the weight of any heavy load, for the load usually would be distributed on such surfaces, besides this, they are mostly immovable and cannot split up easily by the shock of earthquake. Further one of the important features of this particular rock is that it has a special capacity to withstand the lateral thrust which protects the monuments raised on it from even the shock of the earthquakes due to which they had little effect in folding or displacing the original basement of the monument.

Secondly the peninsula have escaped for one reason or another, the weathering of the ages that had cut out all the surrounding parts of the land and are elevated very high from the general surface level of the land. This particular shape is technically known as huge Tors or Block of old plateau. It has helped the builders to save the labour and protected the forts from easy approach of the enemy. Such type of the crust segment is known as "HORST"- a solid crust block or shield which has remained a static land mass of great rigidity and has been unaffected by the folding movement. The forts like Gwalior, Asirgarh, Ajaigarh, Raisen, Ginnor possess such situations and protections.

Thirdly in Indian peninsula these multiple block and basin faulting have attained isolatic adjustment and hence its immunity from major seismic disturbances.

Some of the hills are surrounded by narrow gorges and slopy plateaus which have also played important role in protection of the forts, for instance, the construction of Mandu fort may be quoted here, These gorges have very dark and difficult accesses, however, they have been provided with posterns through steep edges of the slopy hills. Thee difficult gorges were always known to the founders only obviously it was though to trace the access by enemy.

The most essential aspect of forts engineering was to make arrangement of water supply in the forts, Majority of the forts had advanced water supply system. These were connected wither with natural lake, river, streams, nallahs or the tanks built by the founder or they utilised the natural tanks during the planning of the forts. Mostly these were situated inside the top of the hills including the perennial source of supply of water through springs inside the cisterns. The advanced techniques for the supply of water from the natural resources like rivers and streams was also applied by mainly two systems i.e., manual system and syphonic system alongwith Persian wheel system. The water supply system of Asirgarh fort, Mandu, Burhanpur, Narwar, Gwalior, Islamnager forts etc. are a few to quote here where such systems have been adopted. It would be not out of place to mention over here that wherever the artificial tanks were dug by the builders inside the forts they have usually utilised the raw materials taken out of digging for raising the massive walls and buildings, and hence the digging of the tanks played double roles in raising the forts and fortifications. Apart from these the geography of central India had its natural protection by earthquakes because in this part of peninsula no earthquakes have moved which could effect the life of these forts. It is well authenticated fact that majority of the Indian earthquakes have originated from the great plains of India or from the peripherical mountain ranges to their north-west and east. No less than 79 destructive earthquakes have been recorded in this part of India in the last two centuries.[1]

Besides all the above mentioned geographical roles the weather of this part of the country has also played significant role in protecting the forts-for during the monsoon Narmada and Chambal rivers are always flooded and have steep flood and water runs throughout the year due to which it was difficult to cross by the enemies. The major forts like Mandu, Dhar, Gwalior, Asirgarh are situated in the close vicinity of these rivers.

Lastly, the construction of massive fortification walls, bastions etc. was easier in this part of the country because of the availability of rock at particular site of strategic importance which encouraged the patrons to raise the massive structures in a considerably good number.

However, the walls of the forts at Dhar, Mandu and Chanderi etc. are built with different building materials in three distinct vertical layers. For instance, the outer and inner faces are built of blocks of red sand stone and inner core is built by the rubble masonry in local mud, moorum etc.

The gneiss rocks and other types of rocks were readily available and quarried extensively for the use of raising buildings. Specially from

[1] Oldham-List of India earthquakes, M.G.S.I., Vol. XIX, 1983, p. 3.

upper Vindhyan a large quantity of building material was obtained for the construction of building at Ajaigarh, Gwalior, Delhi, Agra, Mandu, and Dhar etc.

In preceding pages, we had a glimpse of geographical position of Madhya Pradesh and the survey revealed that the forts and fortifications were raised on certain specific places of strategic importance. In this context, undoubtedly, geography and climate both played significant roles in raising the defensive monuments.

## Ancient Routes

It would not be out of place to have a review of the ancient routes of the country which were used by the people for their interstate trade relations, pilgrimage and lastly for war purposes. These routes always gave access to invaders for their safe campaign. Some of the major routes of ancient India cannot be overlooked in this context. It is evident that so many natural routes which assumed the character of highways must have played their roles in the history of defense in the contemporary society. During ancient times, India had, undoubtedly, big cities but the majority of the people lived in the villages and hence a major portion of the country was covered with dense forests through which the roads passed. These routes were often infested with wild animals and robbers etc. It was during 6th century B.C. that some of the international routes were known to the people. A few famous routes were as follows :

(A) (1) Sravasti and Pratisthana Route- It was connecting Saket, Kausambi, Arikirn (Eran), Vidisa, Gonarda, Ujjayini, Mahismati and Pratisthana (Ṗaithan) the famous cities of the time for the purpose of trades etc.

(2) Sravasti and Rajagriha Route- This route led from Sravasti to Rajagriha and the major places which connected with this

route were Khapilvastu, Kushinagra, Pawa, Hasthigrama, Bhadagrama, Vaisali, Pataliputra and Nalanda.

(3) Mathura and Vidisha Route- On this route ancient Deograh, Kantipuri, Padmavati and Tumb-ban were situated and were connected with Kausambi also.

(B) The routes through the rivers:

Besides the land routes many routes were also connected through big river, like Ganges and Yamuna etc. through which the trade was carried out by the boats and ships.

The Buddhist literature have mentioned the detailed descriptions of many routes of this period which were used by merchants of Vidisha, Gandhara, Magadha, Sauvira, Bharukachha Suvarna Bhumi and Varanasi etc. These were connected with desert of Rajputana and Marwar, probably, It was connected by land routes also. Panini has also described many places of importance which were connected with routes in Uttarapatha. These places were connected with Caspean sea in the west and the routes of Puruspur to Pataliputra and also to Bahlik, Kapisa Puskalawati, Taxila, Saket, Hashtinapur, Prayag, Kashi, Pataliputra and Tamralipti etc.

It is interesting to mention that many routes were repaired under the Muryas as proved by epigraphic and literary records. It was in Ist century. B.C. when we find the establishments of famous ports in India which connected Roman countries with India, a few of them like Brgukachcha (Bharoncha), Kalyana, Supara, Mujrish are noteworthy, besides Khasur Melgiri, Vijardurg, Paripattan Toggreem and Pattal etc. These routes maintained their importance upto 3rd century A.D. During the Gupta period (300 A.D. to 550 A.D.) we find famous routes like Rajagriha to north west frontiers of India. Famous scholar Kalidasa in his kumarasambhavam has referred to the name of mahapathas and also he has discussed at various places about anupadesa and 18 Islands captured by the king Kartveer. We find the names of famous ports like Tamralipti, Kaveri pattinam of the south in texts. Besides, Bharonch, Paithan, Kasi, Vidisha, Ujjayini, Dasapur, Ahichchhattra, Kausambi, Vaishali maintaining their trade importance. The history of early medieval period is important when we find that the Indian trades continued through sea and rivers and Sindh, Kutch were the famous ports of the period.

The distinguishing feature of the ancient routes was that they were usually connected with ancient capitals and whenever capital was shifted, the routes were also changed to their directions, this was done just because of the varied reasons of commerce, politics, religion as well as the change of the course of rivers and sometimes the whims of the rulers also played role.

Apart from these, we find that these routes had important strategic centres also connected with the large rivers.[1] For, the route of Malwa and Rajasthan crosses the Yamuna at Agra and the route between Bundelkhand and Malwa crosses the same river at Kalpi, and thus obiously the meetin point of the army from Bengal and Uttar Pradesh was in the plain of Buxar (Bihar) after which the river Ganges is wider and it is difficult to cross it. The city of Pataliputra was thus founded considering the safety maesures by its founders. Likewise, south and western India had also some importance of rivers and hills for protection, for instance, the Satpura and Vindhyan hills separate Northern India - Deccan and South. The Vindhyan hills are notable for their natural routes which connected north west and south. Nearly five routes are worth noticing which passed from the east to west. The routes between Punjab and Gujarat passed through Malwa which were followed by conquerors like Mahmood in order to shorten his march route to Saurashtra but the usual and most convenient route was between Sindh and Gujarat through sea only.

1. The strategic points are saltrange between Attock and Jhelum, the plains of Kurukshetra and the hills of Raj Mahal in the vicinity of Bengal and Bihar.

The rivers in the plains flow speedily in rainy season and create impediments in navigation and that is why the dry area of the foot of the hills is followed as the route. The forts raised over the hills were very important for stopping the advance of the enemy. The plain of Kurukshetra is the water shed of basin of Ganga and Sindh that is why this place is most important from the strategic point of view. If the enemy forces proceeding through the Punjab upto Satluj, then the geographical conditions will force him to arrive to the plain of Kurukshetra. The greate war of Kurukshetra was fought here only between the Pandavas and Kaurvas, later on it was place of battle between Prithviraj Chauhan and Muhammad Gouri who fought here at Tarawadi. Once the Mughal laid the foundation of their rule in India from the same plain. The forts in the Gangetic plain may be given the same importance as that of the crossing points of the rivers of Punjab. Centain big cities like Delhi, Agra, Kannauj, Ayodhya, Prayag, Varanasi, Patna and Bhagalpur and of strategic importance. These are established on the banks of rivers and are shelters for protection for crossing points of these rivers.

The route in the Aravali hills connecting Delhi, Ajmer, Ahmedabad cut through central Rajasthan and then following the western foot of Aravali hills reached Ajmer. This is the natural route between Deccan and Rajasthan.

Likewise connecting Mahismati, Ujjayini, Gonardha, Vidisha, Van-Sahva the route reached Kausambi. The Betwa, Tons and Ken were famous rivers located in these routes. By crossing Son and Narmada river one can reach Jabalpur (Javalipur) easily, Ancient Tripuri (Tewar) the capital of the Kalacuris, was situated near this river. The route between Jabalpur and Prayag is indicative of grant route of Bundelkhand. The main route from Jabalpur following Narmada reaches Vidisha and proceeds to modern Itarsi, Hoshangabad, Khandwa. These routes played significant roles in the history of warfare and also for commerce and cultural activities as proved by various epigraphic and literary records. The foreign traveller's accounts, for instance, Alberuni gives some accounts of the routes in western and southern India, out of which the Mathura-Malwa routes in western and southern India, Out of which the Mathura-Malwa route is the same as the Mathura-Dhar route.[1]

In 7th century A.D. Surat-Agra road passed through Sironj and Burhanpur. It was famous for trades between north India and ports of Suraj. From Burhanpur the route passing through Ichhawar and Sehore reaches Sironj and from this route passing Shivpuri, Gwalior, Dholpur reaches to Agra.

The famous city Mahismati was situated on the bank of Narmada at point where Man Singh Gujari ghat of Vindhya and Gandhavghat of Satpura meet to proceed to Deccan. After crossing Satpura hills the route enters to Burhanpur, from there one can proceed to western ghat of Surat and another route going up to Poona valley proceeds to Bevar and Godavary valley.

A few routes which were followed by the Mughal emperors and also by Sher Shah during their campaigns deserve mention over here, Babur (1527 A.D.), the founder of the Mughal dynasty in India, led his troops against Medini Rai, a chief of Malwa and the owner of Chanderi fort, situated in the east of Malwa. He encamped near Chanderi (1528 A.D.) and lastly he negotiated for the peace with the ruler. He might have followed the route from Agra to Gwalior to Shivpuri and then reached Chanderi. It is well known that the throne for the next Mughal ruler- Humayun was not a bed of roses. He had to face serveral enemies in his life and marched extensively in Indian territories to suppress the enemies including his foreign exile after getting a severe defeat from Sher Shah at Chausa (Bihar). Some of the major routes followed by the Mughal army are noteworthy, for instance, Humayun moved from Agra to Gwalior and reached Sarangpur then to Ujjain, a place in the heart of Malwa in 1534 A.D. Afterwards he moved to Mandu and defeated Bahadur Shah of Gujarat also in the same campaign. The capture of Mandu fort itself is a romantic success in the history of the Mughal army under him.[2]

---

[1] Motichandra, Trade and Trade Routes in Ancient India, Delhi, 1977, p.23.

[2] Shrivastav, K.L., 'Mughal Empire', B.V.B. Series, Vol. VII, Bombay, 1974, p.48.

After capturing his area Humayun had certain nefotiations with Bahadur Shah. Lateron, Humayun marched to fortress of Champaner (Gujarat). It was raided by the Mughal army and the fort was captured by Humayun. After this victory Humayun returned to Agra and in July 1537 A.D. he marched from Agra to Chunar (Mirzapur) and then to Patna (Bihar) from where he marched through Teliagarhi to the capital of Bengal and then to Kannauj and lastly he returned to Agra and Delhi.

In 1542 A.D. Sher Shah invaded Malwa after the Size of Gwalior fort, and reached Sarangpur via- Gangron and annexed Vidisha, Ujjain, Dhar, Mandu, Bijagarh and Mandsaur and then returned to Agra via Ranthambhore, and he captured the well known fort of Ranthambhore. It was after this victory when Sher Shah captured Raisen fort and raided Chanderi fort in 1543. After this success he planned to invade Marwar and Jodhpur. He followed the route from Marwar to Ajmer and Mount Abu. The Chittorgarh fort was occupied during this campaign after which the Afghan army moved against Kalanjar fort in November 1544 A.D. Where he had to face severe resistance and was wounded by the explosion. It is said that he died in the camp after his victory.

The above mentioned routes of the Mughal period prove to the fact that generally famous invasions were made by the Mughal rulers with the common routes only.

We may, however, presume that till the fall of the Mughals, who had a very large kindom in India, the main routes were followed for military campaigns and also for trades. It is almost certain that the Marathas also followed the same routes for their invasions on the northern India in general and Madhya Pradesh in particular.

Chapter 2

# THE MONUMENTS

Ancient monument is an historic building that gives us a sense of wonder and makes us a curiosity and want to know more and more about the people and the culture who were the builders.

The monument has architectural, aesthetic, historic, archeological, economic, social and even political, spiritual emotions. The symbolic representation in the monument is another senseful representation.

The monuments are silent listener and speak nothing but spell their past in a lucid way, and with this silent discource that they are celebrating their lives silently apart suffering from number of decaying factors by various harming agencies. these factors are:

(a) Natural factors

(b) External factors

(1) The first destructive agencies that harm slowly are (1) Torrential sains, luxuriant vegetation, seismic distrerbancs, (pisa minar at Itly is an example) salt action, destroy the monument slowly.

(2) Another most destructive effects are the human bandalism and religious fanatism which often led to the disfiguring of monuments

of its rivals. under this catefgory of destructions we may, however include the other factors of robbing of building material for construction of roads, building purpose etc.

It is point out here that many of the antiquaties like Images, decorated panels of stones were utilized for decorating their newly constructed buildings, Amaravati Stupa is an concrete example for this, that the marble decorated slabs and other component parts of the stupa were burnt for preparing fine lime mortar.

Likewise the remains of Mohan Jodaro and Harappa, Bharhut Stupa, were demolished.

**Geology of Stones**

The ancient monuments are built of stones of different varieties, hence the knowledge of geology is essential.

The earth crust in composed of different rocks hard like granite and soft like clay and sand. About 95% of the earth crust is made up of igneous rocks which is composed of granite having felspar, quartz and mica. The remaining 5% of earth crust is made up of sedimentary rocks and metamosphic rocks. Which have been formed from the igneous rocks due to constant chemical and mechanical action of the denuding agents.

**Rocks as Building Material**

Interestingly different varieties of stones are utilized in building the monuments, scattered all over India. In Madhya Pradesh wide range of stones were used in raising the monuments which were locally available, sometimes brought from distant places even.

The geological features of these building materials play main role in disintegration and deterioration of the monuments. For instance, the monuments built of fine grained varieties and without any impurities are in good state of preservation as compared to the monuments built out of coarse grained stones contaminated with injurious ingredients and mineral constituents.

The monuments of the next categories are mostly affected by the atmospheric pollution and hence these are in decaying state of preservations.

The conservation of these monuments have thrown a challenge to the conservationists. Monuments build in different regions may be classified into the following geological categories.

The stone verities of the building in north India are harder and much more resistant against weathering action. They have been obtained from Upper Vindhyan rocks. The majority of monuments at Delhi and its vicinity, viz. Agra, Fatehpur Sikri, Mathura, Sarnath, Allahabad, etc. are built of these stones, besides those in Rajasthan. Some of the rocks of this system provide excellent and durable building material suitable for the use of constructing roofs and floors. It is easier to quarry, to dress and carve and their pleasing and attractive colours have attracted the builders for its use in the finest specimens of Indian architecture, The famous stupas of Sanchi, Bharhut and Sarnath are built of it. The Mughal palaces and mosques of Delhi, Red Fort and even the Rashtrapati Bhawan and the Gateway of India have been constructed with the Vindhyan sandstones. The monuments of Central India (Madhya Pradesh) are constructed with varying varieties of stones; for instance the Parmara temples of Un (Khargone), are decaying fast, having less resisting power against weathering. Same is the case with the monuments at Ujjain and its vicinity.

Interestingly the other monuments of Malwa viz. Dhar and Mandu are built of lameta stones of Malwa plateau. The characteristic feature of these monuments is that they resemble distinct lamination after weathering and salt action. Moreover on account of hydrolysis they become fragile in patches and are easily attacked by cryptogamic growth.

The most delicate and attractive varieties of stone in different shades is utilised in the Parmara's monuments of Bhopal, Vidisha region and the monuments of Pratiharas and Kachhapaghat as in Gwalior region and are stronger against atmospheric pollutions; these are still in a good state of preservation than the monuments of West Nimar. This is because of the homogeneous and non-hygroscopic property of the locally available sandstone of Vindhyan rocks system, and that is why these monuments possess more resisting power against weathering. In these monuments only the superficial strata is affected mildly by carbondioxide and sulpherdioxide gases and a thin film of incrustations is only visible among these as in the Udayeshwar temple at Udaipur, Vidisha and Siva temple at Bhojpur (Raisen).

Another such variety of sandstone of vindhyan rocks have been utilised in the monuments of Bundelkhand region, particularly in the temples of Khajuraho. This variety possess tremendous resisting power and natural plasticity. It can be chiselled easily which facilitated the artisans to give the real expression in the sculptures as well as the ornamentation according to their taste in varying shades. That is why even after centuries they look as a fresh.

The monuments of East Nimar are built of stones of coarser varieties but do not possess comparatively more resisting power and hence they weather easily. The monuments built on the banks of Narmada, as at Bheraghat, Omkareshwar, Barmanghat testify to this point.

The Gondwana and Chhattisgarh regions yield different types of stones which are quarried from upper Gondwana system and used in the monuments. These stones are coarse grained and spongy in nature. The monuments situated in Mandla, Durg, Bilaspur, Rajnandgaon and Bastar districts are badly weathered causing problems for conservation because of the porous nature of stone which becomes granular and the sharp sections are rounded off. Even the chemical treatment creates problems in the long run as at the time of treatment it absorbs the chemicals which reacts with the minerls of inner core and during evaporation it creeps up to the spongy surface of the monument. It is then thrown open to the atmospheric pollutions for further disintegration.

The conservation of temples and monasteries excavated out of the living rock is comparatively more difficult than those of the structural monuments of north and central India. The Rock-cut monuments are excavated in homogeneous rocks and usually the super incumbent mass of rock is supported by massive monolithic pillars. These pillars disintegrate due to weathering action. A number of problems are met with while carrying out conservation of such monuments. This phenomenon is only due to the geological formations of rocks. Such rocks are the Deccan traps. basalt ferruginous in nature, and they get oxidised and are quickly attacked by atmospheric pollutions and thus are foliated. On account of the above property the humid atmosphere in the cave play a catalytic agent in the deterioration nd decay of the rocks. The rock is thus reduced into red, brown and black clay. The ceilings, pillars, images, wall and decorative members show signs of deterioration. The famous Buddhist caves at Ajanta and Buddhist monasteries, Saivite and Jain temples at Ellora are a few examples.

Differing widely from the above caves, are the other caves at Barabar hill and Nagarjuni hill to the north of Gaya (Bihar). These caves have been carved out with infinite labour out of the large boulder like masses of quartzite gneiss. These caves are excavated after the style of wooden architecture and these are still in good state of preservation ever since circa 3rd century B.C. owing to the compact grained variety of stone, Since, this type of stone is of volcanic origin and so hard and compact that even polluted air cannot attack the shining surface of the rock. As it was difficult to excavate the caves on account of the hardness and workability the cave fashioning activity shifted from Bihar to the Western Ghats, where workable stone was readily available.

In the present context the following types of monumental architecture may, however be discussed for our reference.

**A. Type of Architecture**

| | | |
|---|---|---|
| (1) Constructed Architecture | - | Structural Monuments |
| (2) Excavated Architecture | - | Rock cut Monuments |
| (3) Excavated and carved Architecture | - | Monolithic Caves |

**B. Religion Architecture**

| | | |
|---|---|---|
| (1) Hindu Architecture Mathas, Monuments | - | Temples, Pillars, Gates, |
| (2) Islamic Architecture | - | Mosques, Idgah, Dargahs Tombs etc. |
| (3) Buddhist Architecture | - | Stupas, Chaitya Viharas, Caves, Monolithic Pillars |
| (4) Jain Architecture | - | Jain Temple, Gandhakutivihars Religious, Shrines etc. |

| | | |
|---|---|---|
| **C. Secular Architecture** | - | Forts and Palaces |
| **D. Aquatic Architecture** | - | Wells, Tanks, Lakes, Baolies |

The Vedic texts provide us more details about the Aryan and non-Aryan wars and put more emphasis on the forts and fortifications of the period when they entered into India. Most probably, the people who were defeated by these Aryans, during the course of their steady spread were also good builders of the forts and fortified towns but they are not figured in the Rgveda. After the settlement of the Aryans many forts might have been captured by them which are mentioned in these texts. With the role of time the importance of forts and fortifications increased immensely.

It was during sixth century B.C. when the Sodasa-Mahajanapadas were famous for their conflicts for territorial boundaries. Panini has clearly mentioned that the people owed their allegiance to the janapadas with which they belonged.

The Sodasa- Mahajanpadas like Gandhara, Kamboja, Assaka, Vatsa, Avanti, Sursen, Cedi, Malla, Kura, Pancala, Matsya, Vrjji, Anga, Kahsi, Kosala and Magadha were famous during 6th century B.C. Out of these Kahsi was most important and powerful Janapada with its capital at Varanasi. Two kingdoms Kosala and Magadha viewed with each other for the control of the Ganga basin Kali, Kosala, Magadha and Ujjayini confederacy remained important during this period. They fought for political hegemony for nearly 100 years and lastly the Magadhahs emerged meritorious. Bimbisara, the ruler of Magadha had a regular standing army. It was Ajatasatru's time when the conflict between Kosala and Magadha took place after an incident when he killed his father Bimbisara, over which Prasenajita, the maternal uncle of Bimbisara got furious and a war took place. After the death of Prasenajita at Rajagriha the Kosala Kingdom was annexed to Magadha. At Pataliputra the first step was to build a fort which was situated on the Tri-junction of Ganga, Son and Gandaka rivers.

After Ajatasatru, the Nanda dynasty ruled at Magadha most powerful ruler of this family was Mahapadmananda, described in later pauranic works, as the destroyer of all the Kshatriyas, and the first builder of an empire in India.

It was during the first phase of the expansion of power and its consolidation of Magadhan empire a stormy invasion of the most ambitious invader Alexander the Great of Macedon was entered into the Indian land by crossing Hindu Kush in 327 B.C. The contemporary rulers like Ambhi the King of Taxila submitted to him. Porus another ruler was defeated and crushed and other tribes like the Ambastha and Kathas were supressed but the famous Malla tribe resisted from their strongholds, and during the course of fierce conflict Alexander was severely wounded which compelled him to return to his homeland. Thus the great campaign in Northern India lasted for two years and the Nandas of Magadha were avoided on account of their strong position in the fortified town Pataliputra.

Alexander returned but it resulted the establishment of Greek settlement in India. Alexander's whirlwind expedition destructed many tribes but it initiated the merger of the smaller kindoms into bigger ones. Within a few years afterwards, a great general of the time Chandragupta took advantage and became the monarch of Magadhan empire.

Rajagriha which remained the capital of Magadha till the time of Ajatasatru was defended by perimeter of hills and fortified walls.

After the fall of the power of the Nandas three Mauryan rulers were responsible for the unification of the large country under their political suzereignty. The political unification of nearly whole of India (except the extreme south) under the Mauryas was achieved with the help of huge army. The fortification of Pataliputra was a great aid for housing the troops.

The Mauryan rule ended in 180 B.C. and later on the Sungas captured the Major portion of the Mauryan empire. They fought a number of wars in Vidarbha, Northern Deccan etc. In the north-west they fought against the Greeks and in south-east with Kalinga. Most of the tribal states seem to have reasserted themselves under the Sungas, for instance, the Audumbara, Kuninda, Arjunayanas etc. who are establishing their independent kingdoms.

The Kushanas, a Yue-chi-nomads, invaded the country from north-western border and started their encroachment to the Gangetic valley. Meanwhile, during first century B.C. another kingdom of Kalinga gained prominence in political scene under Kharvela. The Hathigumpha inscription throws a vivid light on his military conquests over Rajagriha and Magadha. He repaired his fort immediately after his incarnation.

Towards the fall of the Satavahanas in 3rd century A.D. some tribal states like Abhiras, Kuntalas and Kadambas etc. became powerful. The political history of India ranging from 1st century B.C. to 3rd century A.D. lacked supreme authority. The instability of political atmosphere ended only in 319 A.D. under the Guptas and the whole India was over shadowed by the Magadhan power under the great rulers like Samudragupta and Chandragupta II.

In contrast to the Mauryas, the Guptas do not seem to have possessed a big organised army. The territory's conquered by Samudragupta, during his military expeditions, was mainly due to the troops supplied by his feudatories.

The essential ingredients of the military machinery the elephants, the horses were not housed by the Guptas instead Nardurga was sufficient for them for the military expeditions.

The art of fortifications was evolutionary rather than revolutionary during the rule of Guptas.

The evidence of Chinese pilgrims and the early Muslim chroniclers confirm that the character of the permanent defences constructed around the cities remained during this period. Certain Modifications in dimensions of the walls and ditches were made in the existing forts like that of fort at Pataliputra.

The political supermacy of the Guptas ended in 530 A.D. following the death of Baladitya though his successors continued to rule over Magadha.

## Secular Architecture Forts and Palaces

During the early medieval period in India several Rajput rulers ruled over different parts of India. This period was recognised as the period of political upheaval in Indian history. These rulers had conflicts between them for supremacy and hence it was a period of internecine wars. Many forts of strategic importance were raised by these rulers, for instance, in Northern

India the Kalacuris, Çandellas, Paramaras, Cahmanas, Kachhapaghatas etc. were possessing many forts for their defence. In Madhya Pradesh the forts at Ajaigarh, Kalanjar, Àsirgarh,[1] Gwalior, Narwar, Mandu and Chanderi are a few which played significant role in the history.

For our present scientific study the early, mediaeval forts and their role in making history may, however, be classified as follows:

## 1. THE FORTS OF NORTH INDIA

The forts of North India may be broadly divided into two groups:

(a) The fort at Ajaigarh, Kalanjar, Mahoba, Kannauj, Gwalior, Narwar, Mandu, Dhar, Bijagarh, Chanderi, Raisen etc.

(b) The forts at Purana Quila, Tughlaquabad (Delhi), Kangra fort (Himachal Pradesh), Chittorgarh, Lohagarh, Kumbhalgarh in Rajasthan.

The forts mentioned in 'A' group have played the major role in the history of Northern India during the Rajput period. Now many of these forts have lost their entity but some of them were utilised by the later rulers even during the medieval times. However, the details about the forts of "A" group will be discussed in forthcoming chapters. To quote with the Kalanjar, Ajaigarh, Gwalior and Narwar forts whose roles in the contemporary history cannot be overlooked, particularly under the Gurjar Pratiharas, Çandellas, Kachhapaghatas, and the Cahamanas. Many a times it attracted even the Muslim invaders of Ghazni. The Epigraphic and literary records of the periods referred to these forts invariably indicate their importance. The forts like Kalanjar and Gwalior are supposed to be invisible forts in northern India. The possession of these forts was supposed to be the possession of whole Northern India hence many rulers, even from south, invaded north India with their ambition to capture Kalanjar, Gwalior and Ajaigarh forts,

---

[1] Plate 38 (B).

likewise, the fort at Mandu and Ranthambhore also played the role of key-bolt for the entrance to Indian land for foreigners under the Cahamanas.

It is evident that whenever these forts were captured by the enemies it shadowed the political history of entire Northern India.

It is noteworthy that the Kalanjar fort was invaded by Sultan Mahmud of Ghazni more than once and ultimately the defeat of Hindu King Parmardidev resulted the footings of the Muslim rule in India in 1022. A.D.

The forts enlisted in the group "B" were equally important in the history even during the period of Muslim rulers in India. A few important forts are as follows:

Gwalior Fort, Chittorgarh, Purana Quila, Tughlaquabad, Agra Fort, Kangara Fort, Kumbhalgarh Fort etc.

Gwalior Fort : The story of Gwalior fort goes back to approximately 3rd century A.D.[1] The epigraphic records like Bhoja's Sagar Tal insciption[2] and Ballabhatta Swamins Gwalior inscription prove the fact. During 11th century A.D. it was possessed by the Kachha paghata rulers of Dubakunda branch. The famous Teli-ka-Mandir, Chaturbhuj Mandir (Pratihara period) and the Sasa-Bahu temple[3] raised by the Kachhapaghatas are leaving witness of the Pratihara and Kachhapaghata occupation of the fort.

In 1233 A.D. the Muslim emperor Iltutmis captured the fort and it remained under the Islamic hands tiil 1399 A.D. Afterwards the Tomar King Mansingh set himself on the fort of Gwalior. In 1516 the Tomaras were overthrown by the Mughals who used it as a state prison. The Marathas captured the fort in 1784 A.D. and in 1857 it served as the base in the struggle for independence.

Chittorgarh : This fort was founded in 7th century A.D. and remained the capital of Mewar till 1567 A.D. during the period it was sacked at least

---

[1] Plate 13 (A).

[2] Epigraphia Indica, Vol.1, part I, p. 156.

[3] Plate 15.

three times. i.e., first by Alauddin Khalji in 14th century A.D., then Sher Shah of Gujarat invaded it in 1533 and finally the great Mughal emperor Akbar captured the fort in 1567 A.D., since then it never recovered its previous position. The size of this fort, through the ages, was a glorious history of self immolation of the Rajput men, women and children. The destruction of the fort was the history of the destruction of the brave warriors.

Purna Quila : It is situated on the bank of Jumuna river, the recent archaeological excavations have thrown important light on the construction of the fort in much earlier times. It is proved that the river Jamuna played an important strategic role for the fort.

The Mughal Emperor Humayan remodelled the fort and its massive walls strengthened the bastions along with the fortifications.

Tughalaquabad: The fort was built by the Tukish emperor Ghiyas-ud-din Tughlaque and his son during early quarter of 14th century A.D. Tughalaquabad fortification was completed during 14th century A.D. The fort is octagonal in shape enclosing palace precinct. This fort has a rocky contour and defended by three sides by a deep moat and on the south by a lake. Most probably, it was the centre of Mosoleums under the Tughalaque rulers which is supposed to be the unique example in the history of Muslim architecture in India.

Kangra Fort:[1] It is one of the most impregnable forts in India. It has unique strategic location on a steep rocky summit surrounded by hills. It is also called Red fort of western Himalaya.

The epigraphic records prove that some of the Hindu and Jain temples were raised in 1466 A.D. inside the fort, some inscriptions of 6th, 9th and 10th centruries are available to prove the antiquity of the site. Their famous forts of Himachal Pradesh are Arkle fort, Kam fort, Nurpur fort, Nalgarh fort, Gondla fort, Kuthai fort and Sujanpur fort many of the forts have been converted into hotels.

---

[1] Plate 34.

Kumbhalgarh : It was build by Maharana Kumbha during 1433 to 1468 A.D. It commands a strategic position on some old strong-hold. The founder of this fort Maharana Kumbha witnessed a great service for political developments and invasions and made Mewar more powerful. It was constructed under the supervision of a great following faithfully the guidelines mentioned in the Vastusastras.

## 2. THE FORTS OF SOUTH INDIA

Gingee Fort : The early history of Gingee fort in Tamilnadu is unknown. It is believed to have existed during the period of the Cholas. The history of the fort starts from 3rd century B.C. and continued to circa 18th century A.D. It had gained more importance under the Cholas. The fortifications were completed in 16th century A.D. by Vijay Nagar Kings. The Marathas took over the fort in 1677 A.D. In 18th century A.D. Gingee fort became a bone of contension between the local Princes, the French and the Britishers. In 1750 A.D. the French captured the fort from the Mughals and within 10 years of time it passed on into the hands of English people. The fortress embraces three fortified hills, that form triangle. The citadel dominates Rajgiri the highest hill that forms the appex.

Golkonda Fort:[1] The Rajas of Warangal built the fort in 12th century A.D. In 1363 A.D. it was added to the Bahmanis passing from them the Qutub Shahi Kings in 1518 and remained under them up to 1687 A.D. Golkonda fort was at the height of power fame and importance when it was captured by the last Mughal Emperor Aurangzed who incorporated it in his empire after a 10 year's sieze. The fort stands on a high hill strewn with granite boulders. It is built of megalithic masonry similar to Chittore fort in Rajasthan. Three lines of powerful walls with 76 bastions having buttresses protect the wall. The fort has played important role in the history of South India as well as India as a whole.

---

[1] Plate 38 (A).

Island Fort - Shrirangapattanam : Shrirangapattanam fort was build in 13th century A.D. In 1610 A.D., it became the capital of Mysore Raja till its capture by the British in 1799 A.D. Hyder Ali and his son Tipu Sultan were famous Muslim Kings of the fort who strengthened the fortifications under their supervision. The fort stands on an island washed on both sides by the Kaveri river. It has long straight walls intercepted by the square bastions and surrounded by deep moats of solid granite.

Vellore Fort : Vellore fort is one of the perfect examples of military architecture in India. It was built in 13th century A.D. and by the beginning of 15th century A.D. it became the stronghold of the king of vellore, in 1677 A.D. it was captured by the Marathas. They, too, were ousted in 1708 A.D. by the Muslims who held the fort under their possession till 1768 A.D. Afterwards the British took over the fort. During the period 1778-1781 A.D. Vellore played an active part in Indo-French conflict. The fortress differs in architectural characters from other contemporary forts. It is built on level ground and has double wall projection towards at intervals and the deep wide moatgirds. It has alterations of circa 18th century A.D. Vellore Gopura of Nayakas is situated in the fort.[1]

Fort St. George : It was built by the British in 1653 A.D. on the Madras shore. The fort defied the Mughal and Maratha attempts at Capture but fell to the French in 1745 A.D. The fort enclosed within two lines of wall with wide spaces with the formation of crescent by the moat.

Fort at Chitradurga : It was built in 18th century A.D., during the rule of Muslim rulers Hyder Ali and Tipu Sultan, after 1799. It was garrisoned by the Britishers for a short period. The fort has two lines of powerful fortification with a outwork. It has a picturesque castle from which probably the name derived - Chitrahaladurga, Chitradurga.

---

[1] Plate 37.

## 3. THE FORT OF EAST INDIA

Rajgir Fort : It is said that Ajatasatru built the Rajgir fort. After the parinirvana of Buddha, the fourth Buddhist council was held here. This is supposed to be one of the earliest extent forts in the country Rajgiri may be divided into three parts (i) Rajgiri town (ii) Inter fort containing hot springs. The ruined fortifications of the capital of Magadha still indicate enormous strength and cyclopean proportion They were constructed of rough massive stones.

Rohtasgarh: Rohtasgarh is situated picturesquely on the spur of the Kaimur hill had overlooks the Son valley on one side and a wood amphitheatre of the hills on the other side. Rohtasgarh fort was named after the young prince Rohitaswa. The king Harishchandra the legendry hero of the Hindu Mythology is supposed to built the fort, but the earliest epigraphic record are dated 1169 A.D. probably the period of the foundation of the fort. In 1539 A.D. the fort passed over to the Muslim ruler Sher Shah who built the Jama Masjid and the Musoleum in the fort. Under Man Singh the Viceroy of Bengal and Bihar, a palace and garden were added to the fortification. The Britishers repaired it and finally occupied it.

## 4. THE FORTS OF INDIA (Largest fort of the world Mandu)

Mandu Fort : The hill fort of Mandu (District Dhar) was raised sometimes in circa 6th century A.D. as proved by an inscription engraved on a pedestal of an image of Adinatha discovered from Talanpur near Kukshi in the same district. This record refers to date V.S. 612 (555 A.D.) It was known as Mandapadurga.

Firishta mentons that the fort was built by one tribe king Anandadeo. During 10th century A.D. the fort passed on to the hands of the Gurjar Pratihara kings of Kannauj as substantiated by an inscription found at Pratapgarh (Rajasthan) dated V.S. 1003 (948 A.D.) which refers to the king Mahendrapal of this dynasty. Most probably, the fortifications of the fort were strengthened by the Gurjar- Pratiharas as it played a significant role for protective measures. The fact is further substantiated by another inscription found during the clearance of debris in Dilawar Khan's Mosque.

By the end of 10th century the fort was possessed by the Paramaras of Malwa. Particularly during the reign o celebrated king like Munja and Bhoja. The memory of Munja is still retained with the name of Munja Talao (Tank) situated within the royal enclave. It seems that the later Paramara rulers often visited the fort and resided there for many a times. Obviously, it was more protected than their capital Dhar. Many chiefs under the Paramaras who resided at Mandu paid homage to Udayaditya.

The last Paramara ruler was Mahalak Deo, when Alauddin Khalji captured the fort in 1305 A.D. since then it became the part of the Sultanate of Delhi and Muslim governors ruled over Malwa in 1401 A.D. the fort was captured by Muhammaden governor Dilawar Khan with his capital Dhar. His son Alp Khan shifted his capital from Dhar to Mandu permanently.

In 1531 A.D. it was annexed to Gujarat by Bahadur Shah, it then passed into the hands of the Mughals in 1560 A.D. and remained with them till the Marathas overcame it in 1696 A.D. Lastly it passed to the Dhar family and was later on abondoned.

Daultabad Fort:[1] The hill fort of Daultabad was raised sometimes in circa 12th century A.D. It was one of the powerful seats of capital of Hindu kings- "the Yadavas of Deogiri", known as Deogiri or hill of the Gods. In 1308 A.D. it passed on to the Muslim Sultan of Delhi-Alaud-din Khalji. Mohammad Tughlaue shifted his capital from Delhi to Daultabad and has named it Daultabad- "the city of fortune". Later on, the capital was reshifted back to Delhi. The Bahmanis captured it in the later part of 16th century A.D. and during early part of 17th century A.D. the fort was taken over by the Nizam Shahi kings of Ahmadnagar. It 1636 A.D. the fort was captured by the emperor Shah Jahan and annexed it into the empire of Delhi.

---

[1] Plate 39.

town. A chain of lines of three fortification surrounds the fort, with a number of strong gates. The entrance is through a huge wooden gate flanked by towers. The hillock over which the fort was situated was previously occupied by the Buddhist monks who were meditating in the caves inside the fort.

Murud- Janjir Fort : The sea fort of Janjira near the harbour town of Murud, lies on the west coast of Maharashtra in the beach. It was constructed during 1694-1707 A.D. The fort has battlemented walls, and is built on rocky foundation with 19 bastions containing loopholes for musketry. The fort is in shape. There is a postern gateway on the west which is connected with a wide platform. The Janjira fort had been the most impregnable fort of this coast.

## Cultural Centers of India

With the role of time many of the religions flourished in India. These dynasties established the numerous cultural centres selecting the topographical and geographical set up for the monuments.

These cultural centers amalgamated as the grappling iron that find one generation another. These centers are located

North and Central India.

South India

East and West India

Madhya Pradesh (Central India) being situated in the very heart of India, where considerable number monuments in groups and isolated are scattered right from the prehistoric times to modern, Which played a vital role in building up the glorious history of India.

Madhya Pradesh (Central India) Region

Prehistoric Rockshelters

Protohistoric Remains

Historic Remains of the dynasties viz.

Mauryas

Sungas

Satvahanas and Western Ksatrapas

Nagas

Kushanas

Vakatkas

Guptas

Early Chalukyas (C 500-750AD)

Pratiharas

Western India Rajasthan and Gujarat

**A. Medieval Period of Central India.**

Ҫandellas in Central part of India.

Kalcuries of Dahal in the western part of Central of India

Pamaras of Malwa

Kachchapghatas in northern part of Central India (Gwalior region)

**B. Eastern region of India - Orissa**

**C. Southern region**

Early Chalukyas

Aihole

Badami and Mahakutkeshwar

Patdkal

**Eastern Chalukyas**

Rashtra Kutas

**Western (Later) Chalukyas**

Hoyaslas

Kakatiyas

Pallavas

Early Pandyas

Cholas

Vijai Nagar

Nayakas

**Islamic Region**

Sultanate of Delhi

Mughal Region

Chapter 3

# HISTORICAL BACKGROUND AND ARCHITECTURAL FEATURES OF THE MONUMENTS

## Prehistoric Rock Shelters

The culture of prehistoric man, (neanderthan stage) is called shavar or nishad. The prehistoric man lived in dense forest under the shady trees having thick groves, over the thick branches of tall tress or inside the rock shelters.

The art of rock paintings of Homosepian man, whose skull was developed after a long span of struggle for life but also make the cultural achievement.

This achievement of picturousque rock paintings are found in Vindhyan sand stone hills.

His achievements as a hunter expressing the emotions through dancing his rituals a fire worship scarifies and his hunting a disguised hunter magical rituals for game and marks manship with darts and arrows.

The prehistoric man started this rock painting in Mesolithic period.

This period was regarded as golden age of the development of man. Various kinds of depiction have been discovered in many districts of Madhya Pradesh.

Important Rock Cave Paintings in Madhya Pradesh Adamgarh, Pachmadhi, Churna Gundi and Bori range in district Hoshangabad, Sagar region. Gandhi Sagar Hinglajgarh area (Mandsour district) Shyamla hills, Sahad Karad Dharampuri and Manuyabhan-ki tekri, Bhopal are inspiring Paintings of Bhimbetika[1], Barkheda, Kharbai, Hathitol and Putlikaror in Raisen District.

Abchand, Naryavali and Barakheda in Sagar district Bhimbetka, the biggest rock shelters in the world.

These rock paintings exhibit various colours like red, white, Black, Blue and yellow Hanting scenes, fight of animals, riding scenes, scenes relating to domestic affairs, social life honey collection are the main features that are met with in the rock shelters.

Apart from the above animal like Tiger, Bear, Bison, Bull, Elephant, Boar, Dog, goat, Monkey etc have been painted in the shelters.

Arrows and bows for ceremonial rituals were often decorated. Hunting was the lot of make members[2] of the society, family nourishment was left of female members.

Apart from the above rock paintings of Madhya Pradesh, Prehistoric Caves at Mirzapur (Uttar Pradesh) have also been found where Hunting scene of a wild bore is depicted here, in one of the caves. Likewise sword with handle is represented in fighting scene.

It is to point out here the rock-shelters of Adamgarh depict various scenes of domesticated animals is a rare representation of this region.

---

[1] Plate 1 (A).

[2] Plate 1 (B).

# Protohistoric Remains

Prehistoric art, viz; rock-paintings have been briefly discussed in preceding pages.

The first efflorescence of plastic art can be seen in the Indus valley culture during the 3rd and 4th millennia B.C.

The cultures with its chief centres at Harappa and Mohan-Jodaro was wide spread.

Its remains have been discovered from Punjab in the north to southern parts of Gujarat (Lothal) and from Sind to Meerut (District Saharanpur) Utter Pradesh in the east.

It is to point out here that many other Harappa sites were excavated in India and they revealed many structure including citadel. A few sites like Kalibanga[1] (Hanumangarh Rajasthan), Banwali, Surkotda (Gujarat), Manda, Dadheri, Nagar and Katplan may be quoted here.

Indus Valley art was primitive essentially secular in character. The religious ingredients in some form, however began to appear in that art. It is intestinally to point out here that various dements of Indus valley culture art was borrowed and assimilated after laps of time span in vedic culture.

The vedic symbolism Which become the source material for various art forms in India during proto historic and historic periods was to some extent inspired by the symbology round in the Indus valley art.

Indus Valley art and architecture. The architecture of Mohan Jodaro in general is plain and utilitarian, rather solid than beautiful.

There are no temples as in summer or monumental tombs as on the nile. In contrast to sumer there is an absence of round column were used.

---

[1] Best, R.S. and Ashthana S. - Recently excavated Harrappan site South Asian Aschaeology, Naples 1979- P. 227

The aim of Indus civilization was to make life more comfortable and luxurious rather than refined or artistic.

Harappa is larger in extent than Mohan-Jodaro and had a longer span of life but present nearly the same feature. The careful town planning[1], adequate water supply and efficient drainage, presuppose and advanced state of civil authority was man to the civilization Not only the above pre thought in planning the Indus people had the Sense of sanitation and hygnic. Trees and plants were allowed to grow for fresh and pure air and these people were more cautious about the up gradation of environment.

It was evidently the meeting ground of the people from different parts of Aisa. Sculptural representation also speak of the mingling of diverse races.

Animals were both domesticated and wild. Actual skeletal remains of Indian Humped bull[2], the buffalos the sheep the elephant the pig and camel have been recovered. The Indian humped Ox, "Brahamani bull" is frequently represented in seals the cow and lion was known. Indus script animal human representation[3].

## Historic Remains

### Mauryas

After the fall of Nandas mauryas came into power Chandragupta Maurya was the founder of Maurya dynasty his empire annexed terrtories of Kashmir, Nepal, Bengal, Sindha, Saurastra, Taxila, Baluchistan and Sindh (west) Orisa. Pataliputra being the capital city of ancient Mauryas empire This was a splendid city which draw traders Merchants, scholars and travelers from distant lands.

---

[1] Plate 2 (A).

[2] Plate 2 (B) and 2 (C).

[3] Plate 3 (A) and 3 (B).

The Bharhut stupa of Mauryan period was significant and magnificent heritage building of art and iconography which gained its popularity all over the Buddhist world. At present the remains of stupa are preserved in Indian Museum Calcutta and Allahabad Museum.

Stupa of Amaravati and at Sanchi were the centres of Buddhist activites during 3rd century B.C. The Amaravati Stupa is an ruined state of preservation, reffects, Hinyana sect in theme relating to various incarnation of Buddha, depicting relief of flora, fauna, avifauna and equafauna.

It is to pointout here that the stupa of Sanchi[1] is a little later construction than that of the stupa of Bharhut and Amaravati.

Carving on the railing of stupa of Sanchi depict scrolls, trees, tanks, lakes rivers, animals birds geez etc. depicting Hinayana cult, a symbolic representation that prevailed in the beginning till the carving of images in bold relief was started to their individual concept.

The Monuments depecting Buddhist Murals Paintings are :-

Ajanta Caves, Bagh Caves

Ajanta Buddhist paintings has reached a stage of excellent beauty which migrated to after parts of Buddhist world in later periods such us Bamiyan (in Afghanistan), Tung-human Mangolia in Mangolia or at Sirigriya in Sri Lanka.

It is sad that Bade Buddha in Bamiyan was recently demolished by Talivan. Latter on it is reconstructed by some other agencies of Buddhist faith.

## Monolithic Stone Pillars

Ashoka erected many pillars

1. Sarnath with a capital of four lions
2. Sanchi with a capital of four lions

[1] Plate 4.

3. Rampurwa with a lion capital
4. Rampurwa with bull capital
5. Laubiya Nandan garh with lion capital
6. Lauriya Arasaj
7. Vaishali with lion capital
8. Sankila with lion capital
9. Fragment of bull capital Patna
10. Lion capital in patna Museum
11. Capital with four bulls in Patna Museum

Apart from the monolithic stone pillers, An elephant carved froue the rock eat Dauli in orrisa.

Elephant engraved rock at kalde.

**Rock Edict**

A pillar edict at Sanchi Stupa

Rock edict of Rupnath Jabalpur District

Rock edict of Sonari Ghazikheda

Rock edict at Gujarra District Datia

Rock edicts of Ramgarh hills of Mauryan and Sunga dynasty

It is further intesting to note that the earliest remains of defensive architecture, rock cut cave architecture, stone pillars etc. are the reminants of the past glory of Central India.

The famous centers like Sanchi (ancient Kakanada, Bota-sri-parvata), Besanagar Bodoh pathari, Gyarspur, Ramgarh, Chhapra Tumain (Tumbavan), Kadwaha (ancient- Kadamba Guha) District Guna are a few cultural centers to witness the genesis of the religious and historic art in the region which may, however be traced back to circa 4th century B.C.

Infact Chetiya Giri Mahavihar was attracting the followers of Buddhism in the period of Ashoka the foundation of the great religious establishment at Sanchi, destined to leave a glorious career as an important center of Buddhism for many centuries to come. was probably laid by great Mauryan Emperor Ashoka (Cirea 273-236 B.C.). Who is said to have opened up seven out of eight original stupas erected over the body relics of Buddha and to have distributed the relics among innumerable original stupas built by himself all over his empire.

## Sungas

After the death of Ashoka in 236 B.C. the influence of the Mauryan empire deteriorated the last Mauryan ruler Brihadrath was assassinated by Pushy mitra Sunga in 183 B.C.

Thus sungas followed the rule of the Mauryas. Pusyamitra's eldest son Agnimitra was appointed vice-Roy in Vidisha watch was recognized as the capital of Akar (eastern Malwa). Sungas were ruling and which saw the stone incasing and enlargement of the stupa of Ashoka built in 2nd C.B.C Likewise the erection of balustrades round its ground, berm, stairways and harmica, constructing of temple no 40 and the building of stupa no. 2 and 3.

## Satvahanas

After uprooting the supremacy in eastern malwa Satvahanas came into power. It is to point out here that during the supremacy of satvahanas, new embellishments in the form of elaborately carved gateways[1] were added to stupa 1 and 3.

---

[1] Plate 5.

**Saka-Kashatrapas**

The down fall of the sungs dynasty signalled an alarm for the entry of foreign invaders as there was no paramount sovereign who could weild sovereignty for the large Maghad Kingdom Thus the first great Maghad Kingdom desintriguted into several small political units. The barbaric hordes of sakas, pallavas and Kushanas entered into Indian territory through the north west frontier, the territories of Mathura, Ujjain were held by the saka-Kshatrapas,

**Nagas**

After the decline of the supremacy of Satvahanas Nagas came into power in Akara (Eastern Malwa). The main capital remained vidisha.

Padmavati (Pawaya) Kantipur present Kutwar in District Morena and Earn (District Sagar) were subjugated the other branches of Nagas

Nagas were savaites there is large temple of Dhumeshwar on the bank of river still in good state of Preservation.

Likewise Vatkatakas were also influencing Vidisha region as a center for cultural activities.

**Guptas**

After the decline of Sakas who were ruling Ujjaiyani region from the middle of Second century AD to almost the end of the 4th century A.D. Thus it is obvious that western Kshatrapas maintained their Supremacy for about 250 years over this region till their the sovereignty was crushed by Chandragupta II.

The overwhelming powerful majority of kshatrapas animies like Malva the Abhiraj and Nagas were also responsible for the decline of Saka dynasty and merging into the powerfull Gupta dynasty and thus Guptas become paramount ruler from 4th century A.D. to 7th century A.D.

Allahabad pillar inscription substantiate the fact that number of ruling tribes and dynasties in northern India such a Malavas sankanikas were annexed by Samudragupta.

Later on Samudragupta might have established friendly relations with Nagas. He however married his Son Chandragupta II to Naga princess Kubernaga. According to Erana inscription, Samundra Gupta annexed the territory of Dasarna.

Ramgupta was the successor of Samudragupta and predecessor of Chandragupta II According to many scholars the historicity of Ramgupta become a controversial figure However, the riddle was solved by later discoveries of the copper coins of Ramgupta from Vidisha region and Eran. Scholors like P.L Gupta, A.S. Altekar and K.D. Bajpai attribute these coins to Ramgupta of literary tradition.

Likewise three inscribed image of Jain Tirthankaras which were discovered in Vidisha region (Durjanpur Village) conform the identity of Ramgupta. These inscriptions refers as Maharajadhiraja.

Ramgupta ruled the tract of Dasarn and some parts of Bundelkhand.

It is to point out here that Kumar Gupta- I (414-15 A.D.) Succeeded by Chandragupta II, Who is said to have constructed an image of Tirthankar Parsvanath.

As the Kumar Gupta's health was hempering him to put a strong hold upon his feudatories he was thretend by the Hunas and Pusyamitras. Though his son and successes Skand Gupta Successfully repelled the anemies.

Later Gupta king Buddh Gupta about 495 AD could not put Strong hold over the empire viz. Daśārna region and thus Gupta's lamp of strong hold was extinguished forever.

## Monuments of Gupta Period

Gupta period may be regarded as the golden period in the history, and pioneer in the field of temple construction. For the first time in the history of art and architecture, Gupta period is pioneer in using dressed stones for building temples, prior to this activity of temple construction was made of timber and other perishable materials under the impact of Bhakticult, a large number of temples were constructed under various dynasties in northern and Central India Decan and south regions respectively.

### Gupta temples of Central India at

Sanchi temple No. 17
Bhumra
Sankargarh
Nachna Kuthara
Kari Talai
Deogarh
Khoh
Tigowa
Pathare
Vidisha
Udaigiri
Besanagar
Udaipur
Mandsour
Mukundra
Mahua
Pawaya
Rajim
Sirpur

## Other Sites of Gupta Period

Uttar Pradesh Region

Bhitargaon

Ahichhatra

Kausambi

Gadhwa

Bhita

Deobasarak

Rajgir

Sarnath

## Bihar State Region

Bodhgaya

South India Region

Cheserla (District Krisna)

Aihole (Distt. Bijapur)

Ter (Hydrabad)

## Rock-cut Architecture

Bagh Caves - Distt. Dhar

Rock-cut Cave Ajanta - Aurangabad

Rock-cut Cave at Ellora - Kailas temple

Rock-cut Cave Rani Gumpha (Orissa)

# Development of Style of Temples

Group-I

As discussed in preceding page about the rock cut cave temple half rock cut and half structural the earliest temple at Udaigari and temple no. 17 at Sanchi depict the beginning of style of temple.

Gupta temple at Tigowa (District Jabalpur) and a temple at Eran (Vishnu temple) with an addition of door frame, probably during early Pratihara period (8-9th century A.D.)

Siva temple at sakor (District Damoh)

Siva temple, Bhumra (District Satna)

A brick temple at Baigran (District inajpur) East Pakistan is Similar in design as temple at Bhumra.

Group-II

The second group of temples characterized by the addition of roofed ambulatory round the sanctum.

Parvati temple at Nachna (District Panna)

Group-III

The third group of temples distinguished by the presence of spire (Sikhara) over the square sanctum (Garbha-griha) Dashavatar temple at Deogarh Jhansi is an unique example.

Temple at Bhitargaon (District Kanpur) belong to North Indian style of temple, constructed of brick and terra cotta, tri-rath construction with prominent central offset a sanctum and ardha mandapa (ante- room) corbelled ceiling domical vault.

Bodhgaya Temple - District Gaya

The original brick built Mahabodhi temple[1] is roughly coeval with Bhitargaon temple, Bodhgaya temple enshrining an image of lord Buddha in Bhumisparsa mudra in the sanctum.

Post Gupta temple

Lakshaman temple at Sirpur, District Raipur a brick construction of 7th century A.D. likewise a good number of brick temples are located in Chhattisgarh region. At Sirpur a star type temple in ruined state is located here. At Nalanda (Bihar) a temple is known as Stupa-Sila (iii) belong to 6th century A.D.

Makandra (Kota, Rajasthan)

Ramgrah (District Shahabad, Bihar)

Group-IV Rectangular temple (Shrine): apsidal rear end and vagon vault roof showing a gable-end Chaitya dormer design, viz; Ter (District Sholapur, Maharashtra) Cheserla (District Krisna, Andhra Pradesh) both of brick masonry structure raised.

Pawaya is excavated brick temple terraced (Distt. Gwalior)

Such types of temples have been unearthed at Aichchatra (Ramnagar in District Barelly and Paharpur (East Pakistan)

Temples of later Gupta period (7-8 the C.A.D.) are

Ramgarh

Chhapara

Badoh All in District Vidisha

---

[1] Plate 8.

Gupta temples of slightly later date are situated at Kundalpur District Damoh Mahua (District Shivpuri).

It is interesting to mention that the construction of temple by stone in Gupta period initiated an epoch of temple construction, with simple square sanctum and four pilled portico to sikhara style of temples upto 7-8th century AD and a little later is a significant feature of unity of various dynasties of India in general and central India in particular is a vision of Hormony of monument.

The Brahmanical temple is regarded to be the most prolific architecture in India. The greater vigour in the development of this activity can be noticed more easily than in any other architectural form.

Temple building was taken up as a cultural movement all over the country during the Gupta period. Architectural remains of Brahmanical temple prior to Gupta period have hardly survived, except a few extant remains.

The Indian temple sites are urthas and ksetras, where a potent presence is felt to dwell. The Gods are seen at play at such a site where groves are near rivers, mountains, springs and in towns with pleasure gardens.

In recent excavation at Besanagar, Vidisha an apsidal plan of a Vasudeva temple belonging to circa 2nd century B.C. has been found displaying the quality of material used and remarkable constructional techniques.The existence of the temple is authenticated by Heliodoros Pillar inscription at Besanagar.

This is the earliest structural activity of temple construction so far found in Malwa region.

The period between circa 400 A.D. - 750 A.D. was the classical period of Gupta architecture, and this was preceded by a phase of rich timber architecture (circa 200 B.C. to 400 A.D.).

The epigraphic records prove that the Gupta dynasty played a dynamic role in building the Brahmanic shrines.

The inscription on the back wall of the "Tawa cave" at Udaigiri is the first information about an excavated temple shrine dedicated to Siva (Sambhorgguham) in circa 400 A.D. by Virsena, the Minister of Chandragupta II.

Likewise the Dasapura inscription of Bandhuvarman of the time of Kumargupta records the erection of a sun temple as lofty as Kailasa mountain (Kailastunga sikhara pratimani).[5]

Owing to the favourable geographical environment and historical reasons, a large number of well preserved Gupta temples are located in Madhya Pradesh viz, the monumnets at Udaigiri, Sanchi, Tighwa, Bhumra, Pathari Eran, Kunda, Khoh Nachna Kuthara Kari-talai, Mandsaur, Deogarh, Sirpur etc.

The early architects of the Gupta period had a clear idea about using a cubical block to establish the Siva temple such as the Tawa cave Temple" at Udaigiri, with a plain sanctum on a square plan, with a lotus ceiling.

The architects do not appear to have been confident about the loading conditions of a structural temple. That is why they first experimented with a partly excavated and partly structural temple at Udaigri cave No. 1 (False Cave). Here they excavated a rectangular sanctum (7'x6'), providing plain square pillars with wider intercolumniation in front of the mandapa of 7 ft. square in plan, one of the sides being built up by cutstone masonry, the roof of the mandapa being a natural ledge of rock. The spacing of the pillars was adjusted with a view to distribute the unsymmetrical dead load of the natural ledge of rock, to the base of foundation.

As a result of the experiment of Vidisha craftsmen with structural activity at Udaigiri in circa 400 A.D. construction of a full fledged structural temple made of ashlar stone masonry become possible in 5th century A.D. at Sanchi for the first time.

Undoubtedly, Udaigiri temple site may be regarded as the forerunner in the development of the Gupta temple architecture, and Chandragutpa II, King was the pioneer in this activity in Malwa region.

It is obvious that in raising structural temples, architects of Gupta period followed the square plan theory of "Vastupurusamandala" forming a well defined cube, covered by a flat ceiling simply supported on walls and pillars.

Structurally a cube is always stable and remains in equilibrium condition, as its centre of gravity i.e. axis line passes through the centroid of the base area.

All the temples belonging to the Gupta period possess some common architectural and sculptural features typical of the age, in corporated from canons of vastu texts.

The most striking characteristic features of Gupta temple, recorded by Cunningham during the survey of Malwa and Bundelkhand in circa 1874-1877 A.D. are as follows.

1. Flat roof without spires.
2. Prolongation of the door lintel beyond the end of the jambs.
3. Statues of the river Goddess Ganga and Yamuna guarding the entrance door.
4. Continuation of the architrave of the portion as a moulding all round the building.
5. Pillars with massive square capitals ornamented with half seated lions back to back with a tree between them.
6. Bosses on the capitals of a peculiar form, like beehives with short side horns.
7. Deviation in plan from the cardinal points.
8. Of the facade, the intercolumniation in the middle being wider.

The site for construction of the temples was chosen at a comparatively higher altitude than the normal ground level, possessing high bearing capacity and non porosity of the foundation strata.

Chisel dressed cut stone masonry of lofty blocks of fine grained, homogeneous, sedimentrary rocks have been usd in raising the plinth wall, super imposing the rubble filling in the foundation.

The damp proof course masonry of stone band projecting out ward having lamination at right angles to the super structure have been incorporated. This device is adopted to protect the super structure of the temple from deterioration by the capillary action of water creeping through broken joints of the masonry.

The super-structure is raised from chisel dressed fine grained small stone block of varying sizes, by percussion method devoid of any morter. The five faces of blocks of stones are chisel dressed leaving the inner face rough tooled.

The continuation of the moulded architrave of the mandapa and outer facades of the sanctum is functional as D.P.C. of the plinth structure wall. The stone slab with outlet conduits over the sanctum may be taken as a beam of simply supported rectangular section, carrying uniformly distributed load per unit run over the whole span. It remains within safe limits of shearing forces and bending moments. The load is equally transmitted through super structure over the foundation wall, as the area of the base of the sanctum of the temple is square.

The sanctum of Sanchi temple No. 17 is square (8' 2" x 8'2") while the mandapa is rectangular. The uniformly distributed load of the slab is sustained properly by four square pillars of requisite height, intercolumniation in the middle being wider and forming a square plan of slab. Thus the central concentrated axial load is distributed by the trabeate door by prolongation of the door lintel beyond conditions the structure becomes stable and stays in axial alignment.

An analogy of such intercolumniation is seen inside the rock cut caves, mandapas and even porches of the temples of later period viz. Çandellas, Paramaras, Kalacuris etc. The temples at Khajuraho, Udaipur and Bhoramdeo are a few monuments to quote here. In the Siva temple at Bhojpur we see the above type of spacing of the pillars even inside the sanctum.

On account of the larger area of Garbhagrha the pillars forming the main elements of the frontage of the Gupta temple may be termed as those of early Gupta "Order". The components of the pillar are (a) A plain square pedestal (b) a short shaft of many sides (c) a capital esembling a broad conventional vase (d) a massive abacus surmounted by a device of lions and tree motif.

Noteworthy is the fact that the dimensions of the pillar are designed according to the dead load of the area of roof and crushing strength, per unit run. The axis of the Load line passes axially through the centroid of the square pedestal of pillar.

In case of Rock-cut caves homogeneous massive pillars have been excavated in varying designs with square or circular base pedestal according to the unsymmetrical land of the surmounting rock area.

The architects of Gupta period were not satisfied with flat roof construction of temple. They were perhaps imagining for a sikhara type of temple and hence the slabs of smaller size were placed one over the other forming a receding tier sikhara taking into account the axial alignment.

The next stage is met with at Deogarh where three staged pyramidal sikhara was raised in gradually receding tiers. In such cases the area of base in increased by projections on four sides.

Deogarh temple among the Gupta temples is conspicuous as it represents the first known sikhara type temple in northern India.

1. Brhat Samhita, LV, pp. 4-8, Bhavisya Purana, I c XXX, pp. 11-15.

2. Brown, Percy, Indian Architecture : Buddhist and Hindu, pp. 37, 44, Kramrisch, Stella, The Hindu Temple, pp. 109.
3. Warner Spenser, Thomas and Hudson, Oriental Architecture in colour, pp. 275-76.
4. Fleet, C.I.I., Vol. III, p.34
5. C.I..I, III, p. 81.
6. Cunningham, A.S.R., Vol. X, p. 60
7. Ibid, Vol. IX, p. 42

## Site of Early Chalukyan temple (C 500-750 A.D.)

The principle sites for the constriction of early Chalukyan temple are

Aihole

Badami

Mahakutkeshwar

Pattadakal

The above sites of group of temples situated within a few kilometers apart in district Bijapur of Mysore state.

This temple building construction was contemporory to the temple construction of Gupta dynasty the earliest temple of 5th C.A.D. is temple no 17 of near Sanchi stupa No.1.

The early Chalukyan temple construction activity began in 5th century A.D. and ended about the A.D.

The earliest temple of this region is Ladh Khan at Aihole, 13 km. from Pattadakal.

Various temples represent prototype of North Indian type of temples.

Mahakutkeshwar group of temples are situated close to Badami Known as Sangameshwara and Virupaksha temple comprising a sanctum and portico, highly decorated with niches in four cordinal offset by images. the temple is adroned with a stumpy and massive sikhara, resembling the early temples at Aihole.[1] Regarding the last and latest Chalukyan centre at pattadkal, the temple style's coupled together with both northern and southern style fusing together. So far as the nottern style temples like Kadasiddheswar and Jambulinga, is concerned, they are the simplest, possessing only a sanctum and a mandapa. The sanctum of each being crowned by a squate and Panderous shekhara.

The sanctum of each is adorned with nich at bhadra-projections by one relief sculpture respectively.

Likewise the Kashiviswanath temple is similar in plan to the above mentioned temple, except its sikhara is in advanced stage by having a Pancha-ratha variety, divided into five stories, and its mandapa is a flat roofed consisting two tiers.

The temple of Papanath situated close to the above temples mentioned above is long low structure consisting a porch, Maha-Mandapa, vestibule and a garbha-griha. The last one being adorned by a stunted nothern type of sikhara.

The unbalanced and inorganic plan and design, the temple indicate that it is still in a formative and experimental stage.

A group of nine temples are situated on the bank of river tungabhadra in Alampur, district Mahabub Nagar near Hydrabad. These temples are popularly known as the Nava Brahma temples, eight of them possess North Indian style (early pratihara style of architecture), while nineth of them belong to the south Indian style. The temples situated in groups mentioned above the Savagra Brahma temple contain an incription of Chalukyan vijaya

---

[1] Krishna Deva Temples of North India p. 18.

datya (696-733 A.D.) of Badami family and Kumar Brahma mentions a Vallabha, the well known virud of the early Chalakyan kings.

It is therefore, appear that these all groups of temples were raised by the early Chalukyan rulers of Badami during (7-8th) century A.D.

## The Pratihara Temple of Central India

Temples of pratihara have been divided into three phases First phase (Circa 725-780 A.D.) Second Phase (Circa 800-850 A.D.) Third Phase (Circa 850-900 A.D.) The art of the temple of Pratihara period in Central India serves as a transition between the post Gupta art and the medieval dynastic art of Northern and Central India.

The temple construction during (8-9th century A.D., Surviving in central India and Rajasthan posses common feature which distinguish them from the preceding and succeeding theistic building.

The temple construction activity prominent in the above regions where the gurjara Pratihara dynasty (8th-9th century A.D.) was ruling. Since the pratihara extensive empire from Kannauj ruling over an extensive part of central India, including Uttar Pradesh and the Punjab as well as the Himalayas and upto east and west regions.

The pratihara temple style of central India is reconed by a low Adhistan with simple stunted sikhara well decorated with single band of images fitted within niches crowned by udgamas and modest plan, consisting of only the Garbhagrah, antral (vestibule) and Ardhamandapas.

The pratihara temples of Rajasthan situated in groups as at osian have a more eleborate plan and slightly different design and decorative carvings.

Since there temples play a vital role in the development of regional style in central India is a noteworthy feature.

A group of temple at Naresar in Gwalior region, provide us a sequential development of temple architure in stages, Likewise the pratihara temples of Bandhogarh fort (District Satna) provide us a feature of development of temple architecture at one place.

The style of these temples show a square sanctum with a curvilinear tri-rath sikhara of stunted shape and constricted vestibule covered by a gabled roof. The Dwarsakhas are of over door design usually with three simple Sukanasikas Sakhas, decorated with scrolls Slhambha Sakha (Pilasters) and Nagsakha whose tails are held by Garuda, represented centrally on (Lalat Vimb) The lintel is represented by arches composed of bold Chaityas, Surmounted by a frieze of chain and bell design all round the temple as a whole.

The Jangha is plain except the Bhadras, depicting deties viz. Ganesh, Karikeya, Lakulisha, Surya and Parvati.

Likewise the group of temples at Batesara district Morena and Mahadev temple at Amrol near Gwalior are similar on plan the later being slightly larger consisting of relief carvings.

The Amrol temple conttains decorated sculptured nich on each projection with a bold Udgama.

The sculptures representing parivara of Śiva and Ganas. These temples anticipate the Teli-ka-Mandir in Gwalior fort and are 8th century A.D. old.

The Śiva temple situated at Mahua, district Shivpuri is identical in plan with that of Amrol temple, showing slight deviation in details of design and ornamentation. This temple replaces the kalash moulding of the Adhisthan on the central offset (Bhadra bathika) by ornate square rafter-ends design, a feature characteristic of central India from earlier times.

The Jangha shows a prominent nich is confined to the bhadra, the reaming projection being plain but are continued by square pilasters with a few ornaments viz Ghata Pallav, lows vandh and foliage band a typical pratihara style.

A small temple at Terahi very close to Mahua is a later period construction, contain panch rath sanctum in advanced plan.

The Teli-ka Mandir in Gwalior fort is the grandest temple of Pratihara style with an exceptional design, having a vagon vault (Shal- Shikhara) Superstructure[1].

The temple is entered through a grand flight of steps leading to an elaborate doorway of five bands.

River goddess flanked by S'aiva dwarpalas The temple is dedicated to shakti. According to an inscription and its paleography indicate its date of construction C. 850 A.D. during pratihara king Mihera Bhoja (836-888 A.D.).

It is to point out here that a Śiva temple situated Indor (District Guna) possess a similarity with Teli-ka Mandir.

Later temple architecture flourished after the above temple, Jarai Math at Barua Sagar destic Jhansi and Gadarmal temple at Badoh (District Vidisha) contains labiously carved mandapa pillars and a little more evolved on plan and in desin that the other pratihara temples discussed in preceding pages.

The Chandramukh Mahadeo Temple at Nachna (District Panna) carries over its garbha griha a deeloped Northern Shikhar of pancha ratha design. The decorative architectural motifs, like the pediments Tamal Patra flowers garland loops and square rafter - end carved with conventional lion heads are the developed pratihara style of the 9th C.A.D.

The Kutakeshwar temple at Pathari (District Vidisha) consisting of Kadamba type of tri-ratha pyramidical shikhara a pidhas a constricted vestibule and porch of single way similar to the Rock-cut, Chaturbhuja temple left side of Gwalior fort gateway. Both these temples belong to the 9th C.A.D.

The Jaina temples No. 12 and 15 at Deogarh (District Jhansi) are best preserved and belong to 9th C.A.D. The Navranga Mandapa of temple

---

[1] Plate 13 (B).

No. 15 is a Sandhara type temple. Its sanctums pancha-rath on plan and adorned with a heavy Shikhara.

The Mala Devi temple at Gyaraspur (District Vidisha) is partly Rock-cut and partly structura!. It is a mature example of temple architecture of pratihara period.

The roofs of the temple of the porch and mandapa (The hall) are pyramicial composed of horizontal tiers. From engineering point of view the load of structure from north side the rock is utilised as load bearing.

The partihara temples of central India are thus seen to have a simple plan and design displaying some characteristic Ornaments of the style, including tall pediments a friez of garlands loops on the top of the wall, a band of Nagas on the door frame and rich carvings of vase foliage, scrolls, kirti nukhas and square ribbed cushion capitals including rafter - end designs are the features of Pratihara architecture.

Likewise there are a few pratihara temple in Kullu Himachal Pradesh belonging to early 8th C.A.D. namely Jagatsukh (near Mandi Kullu, Himachal Pradesh Gopeshwar Shiv temple and Lakhamandal and is among the earliest examples of pratihara style, with its simple triratha Sanctum resembling that of the Naresar group of temples, roofed by a "Shikha" and Chaitya- dormers.

Gopeshwar and Jageshwat temples, resemble that of the Teli-ka Mandir. Basheshwar temple at Bajaura (District Kullu) has an advanced plan and architectural design with a four faced opening and has elongated statuary the regional art style.

Apart from the above temples there are a few temples in chamba region namely Shakti Devi at Chhatrahi and of Lakshana Devi at Brahmaour are worth Mention.

These are the earliest surviving wooden shrines depicting a rich repertoire ot pratihara ornaments and decorative motifs with some influence of Gandhara style and arts of Nepal and Kashmir.

Likewise at Masrur (District Kangra) these is a Rock-cut complex belonging to half of the 9th century A.D. is a notable pratihara monument of art and architecture.

## Temples of Western India

One of the earliest temple known as Shitaleshwar temple situated at Chandravati near Jhalarapatan (District Jhalawar) in Rajasthan, belongs to 689 A.D. The temple at present contains a sanctum (Garbha griha) and an (Antaral) Vestibule, which are roofless. podium (Jagati) mouldings are bold and simple.

The sanctum has prominent nich shrines on the coordinal offsets. The pilasters are well decorated with vase and foliage motif at the base and capital. Ganga and Yamuna are represented in sculptural tradition of the Gupta period on its lower part.

Likewise the Śiva temple at Kansua (District Kota) bearing an inscription in 738 A.D. Looking to the features of this temple it is identical in plan and design to the temple mentioned above i.e. shitaleshwar temple.

The temples like Harshat-Mata temple at Abanri (District Jaipur) and another temple at Mandor (District Jodhpur) are in bad state of preservation.

One of the important group of temples at Osian (District Jodhpur) may, however be divided into series.

The earliest series of group of temples are nearly a dozen ones. Likewise later group of temples are 6 in numbers.

The earlier group of temples are well covered in decoration and architectural peculiarities. These temples raised over a high platform (Jagati) Containing bold relief carvings of floral designs.

Noteworthy features of the temples are that they are pancha-ratha on plan and in elevation and show sculpture nich on all the five rathas

(Projections). These deties are Narsinha Trivikram, Varah-Vishnu, Harihara on the Vaishnav temples.

Harihara sun temples are well decorated with interlacing design of adorning Nagas, whose tail are held by in the hands of Garuda.

The ceilings of both vestibule and Mandapa are well carved with Nagapasha entwining Vidyadharar. Apart from the above templs, the Mahaveera Jain temple which was built during the reign of pratihara vatsaraj (783-92), Which is corroborated by inscription on the temple.

So far as the art of the temples at Osian are Concerned the earlier temples are Characterized by voluminous modelling and rich iconography.

From the art and iconographical point of view these temples resemble with the early pratihara temples of central India as discussed in preceding pages and thus the Osian temples belong to 8th Century A.D.[1]

Likewise the later group of Osian temples belong approximately 10th-11th Century A.D.

## The other temples

Sachiya-Mata Temple - 12th C.A.D.

Kalika Mata temple at Chttorgarh - 8th C.A.D.

Kumbhashyama temple at Chittorgarh

Śiva temple at Buchkala, Distt. Jodhpur

Vishnu temple at Buchkala Distt. Jodhpur

(built by Pratihara King Nagbhatta II in 815 A.D.)

Kameshwar temple at Auwa (Distt. Pali in Marwar)

Sun temple at Varman (Distt. Sirohi)

Ghanteshwar temple at Budoli (Distt. Udaipur)

Ambika Mata temple at Jagat (Distt. Udaipur)

Durga temple at Unwas, Udaipur region, 10th C.A.D.

Mahavira temple near Ghanerao (Distt. Pali) 10th C.A.D.

Nilakantheswar termple at Kekind (Distt. Nagaur)

Lakulisha temple at Ekalinga (Distt. Udaipur)

Vaishnava temples called Sas - Bahu at Nagda (Distt. Udaipur)

Mir and Mahadeo Temple at Ahar (Distt. Udaipur)

Someshwar temple at Distt. Barmer of Marwar

Well developed temples, 10th -11th C.A.D. During 12th C.A.D. a substential part of Rajasthan including Marwar and Mewar, passed under the sovereingty of Solanki of Gujarat. Thus these areas of Rajasthan become a province of Solanki style Solanki style of temples are at

Chittor, Ekalingaji, Jalor and Ranakpur, Scattered in deferent part of Rajasthan.

The climax of the medieval architecture of the Rajasthan and Solanki Styles was reached in the dilwara group of Jain temples at Mount Abu,[1] of which most important are Vimala Vasahi and Dona Vashi built in 1031 and 1230 A.D. The stove carvings in door frames niches pillars architecture and ceilings are elegant and super among the temples of India. The temple construction of solanki style reached, to its climax upto 15th C.A.D. Kriti Stambha (Tower of fame) at Chittorgarh built by Rama Kumbha (1440-1498 A.D.) and Jain Chaumukha temple at Ranakpur Distt. Pali dated 1438.

The temple construction become a distinctive feature of western region of Gujarat region one of the richest regional style of North Indian temple architecture. This region in case of temple construction under the powerful rulers of solanki dynasty had a most prolific development in

[1] Plate 17 ceiling of Vimala Vashali.

temple architecture. The shrine at Gop (District Jamnagar of Saurashtra) belonging 6th century A.D. may be regarded as the earliest monument of western India.

The sanctum of the Gop Shrine has a unique features of architecture which are distinctly seen that are exhibited by more than fifty surviving examples in Saurashtra.

Distinguished by a simple plan and design with a tall featureless wall, with diminishing a number of Chaitya dormers, with roof of puramedical stepped courses.

These shrines belong to 6th C.A.D. and are peculiar to this region. It is to point out here that the temples raised in this region during 6th century A.D, may however be regarded as pre solanki architecture.

The Bhansara group of temples and temple at miani built in district Junagarh contains three stepped courses in formation of roofs.

In the above process of construction four stepped. Tiers decorated with Chaityas dormer, four on the lowest to one on the topmost tiers have been constructed. The example of such a type of temples are Khimeshwar (District Jamnagar) and Kalsur (District Bhavnagar) respectively.

The temple of Pindara and Navidhrewd (District Jamnagar) Contain roof of 5 similar tiers with Amalak at the corners.

The largest example of the above temples discussed above is at 'leshwar (District Junagarh) superstructure is constructed with a tall ımid of six tiers, on the corner sides are cupola life finial superimposed ıala savakas with pot finial.

'e sun temple at surapada, situated near Prabhas patan, possess a type of sikhara, a Sandhar type of construction this temple belongs '0 A.D.

ɜe the group of temples situated at Roda, resemble early partihara ıp of temples at Nasersar Gwalior region.

The monument of solanki dynesty of this region belonging to early circa 11th C.A.D. are Someshwar temple at Gorad, situated Śiva temple at Sandar, Mata temple at Dhinoj in district Mehsana are good example of large architectural temples.

Nilkantha Mahadeo temples at Sunak is the superfine full developed temple architecture of late 11th century A.D. construction of solanki dynasty.

Dugdheshwat temple at Madropur (Distt. Kheralu) ad Lakulisa temple at Pavgarh (District- Baroda) reflect the Malwas style of temple architecture.

It is intesting to point out here that the intensive carving stone activity was promul gated in Gujarat region by the Siddharaj Jayasimha (1094-1143 A.D.) a paramount ruler of solanki dynesty than in other part of India.

Note worthy are the temples viz Navalakha temple, Rudra mata temple, (situated on the bank of Saraswati river) at Viramgan may be asigned a super value construction activity the during 12th century A.D.

The large and small temples, displaying the chrematistic decorative and plastic ornament of style of foliage flora and fauna depictions attract the visitors and scholars possessing of the temple architecture tastes.

A great emphasis of building activity was maintained during the 13th century A.D. and a few temples were constructed here somewhat resembling the architecutral features of Sas-Bahu temples of the Gwalior fort.

## Jain Temples

Among the solanki rulers, who were having Jain faith, they raised many jain shrines, on the sacred hills of shatrunjaya and girnar in saurashtra region. viz triple - Shrined temple of Adinath at Girnar (District Junagarh is worth mention).

Likewise the colosal Jain temple at Taranga (District Mehsana) is most splendid and impressive of its size and architecture.

A few Jain temples at Ranakpur (Distt. Pali, Rajasthan) are good specimen for traditional architecture of Gujarat and Rajasthan Which flourished in this region during 15-16 the A.D.

It is to mention over here that a group of Jain temples at Kumbhariaji (District Banaskantha) were constructed during 11th century A.D. at Mount Abu, Delwara.[1]

These temple were constructed by marble stones fine specimen of carving and Iconographical features, as discussed in preceding pages.

---

[1] Plate 16.

Chapter 4

# ART AND ARCHITECTURAL DISPOSITION OF MEDIEVAL MONUMENTS OF CENTRAL INDIA

In preceding pages early temples of Indian history, have already been discussed in details. Madhya Pradesh being situated in the heart of India and the topographical and geographical features of this region was as such, that it was open to influences from all sides. The powerful rulers who ruled over the region during medieval period are.

The Çandellas of Jajak bhukti, Kachhapghatas of Gwalior, the parmaras of Malwa and Kalcuries of Tripuri (Jabalpur, District) being the major ones.

These powerful rulers competed with one another in the arts of war and peace and surveyed the monuments with which the central India was once thickly studded. The harmoneous attitude of these powerul rulers reflected in the field of construction of monuments.

The Gupta art and architecture were Kept up by the Pratiharas as discussed the preceding pages.

The Gupta and Pratihara legacies being common to all of them, this resulted that the constructional features of the monuments shared in plan and design and decorative scheme.

This phenomenon is a testimony of a vision of harmony of monuments.[1] Among the common constituents in planning the building temples are the Garbhgriha (the sanctum), Vestibule (Antaral) and Hall (Mandapa).

In the development scheme of the temple construction the Mandapa has lateral transepts and a porch (Ardh mandapa) in front is partly enclosed by ornamental balastrade which is canopied by over hanging eaves. The Suknasa antefix is of the stepped and gabled design and carries usually an image of rampant lion.

The height of Sikhara ovet the sanctum may vary from 5 to 7 rathas, the last being tappered up to form a neek fixing two amalasarkas the upper being smaller with a hole for crowning a potfinial.

So far as the decorative features of the temple is concerned that the foliage designs and scrolls etc. are incised like a stencil cut, are distinctive features of temples of central India.

The temples of paramara of Malwa depict a pronouncedly individual features of design of temples which were influenced by the art and architecture of adjoining territories of Rajasthan and the upper Deccan and maintaining contacts with Khandesh and Konkan, which were annexed by the parmaras.

This the parmaras style of constuction of temples of central India may be treated under the monuments of the Decani style.

We may mention some of the individual temple architecture that flourishedin the Tapti region and upper branch of the Krishna on south.

# Ajanta Caves

It is to mention over that at Ajanta[1] in Deccan, out of 30 rock caves consisting of two Chaitya-halls (9 and 10) four viharas (Nos 8, 12, 13 and 30) are early group of Rock-cut monument and of the same type as Buddhist Rock-cut excavation at Bhaja, Karle, Kondane, Pital Khora, Nasik, Kanheri, belonging to a period second century B.C. to the second century A.D. The rest of the caves belong to the perod after fourth century A.D. these caves were excavated during Vatakas (450 and 600 A.D.) The last ones were excavated around 650 A.D.

The Rock-cut activity continued till the times of the Rashtrakutas in the 8th 9th century A.D.

So far as the early chaityas are concern they are large, aspidal, with an elaborate facade, having horse shoe-shaped windows on the top of the entrance and the interior divided into a central nave and lateral aisles by two rows of columns. The aisles continude all round the apse as circumbulatory passage. A Rock-cut stupa in the apse portion a centre of attraction of worship object. The ceiling being flat or vaulted. The Rock architecture of the second phase consists of two aspidal Chaityas (19 and 26) thus these abodes of stone, or hill-abodes called Sailgriha in an inscription datable between 450 and 525 A.D. in cave no. 26. Which is a Vihara Chaityas.

Likewise the Buddhist Rock-cut architecture of Ellora, containing twelve Rock-cut caves 1,2,3 and 5 dating from fourth century A.D. cave No. 4 and from 6 to 10 are asignable to 6th century A.D. respectively. Cave no. 11 and 12 are unique caves and belong to 7th century A.D.

The caves temples at Aurangabad include a Chaitya of the earlier Hinyana phase and a number of Viharas and other belonging to 7th century A.D. are of less importance among the Rock-cut groups discussed above.

The Mural Paintings of Ajanta are superve as the celebrated paintings created by monks, by varigated colours.

---

[1] Plate 7.

The Rock-cut activities was already prevent in Ajanta and Ellora and in due course of time his activity was going to end. The architects wanted new style of construction as they were tired of the Rock-cut activities.

It provided an inspiration to a new structural movement of its own significant this structural feature is its sikhara of "Bhumija class" with four spines decorated with the usual mesha of Chaitya dormers on the central rathas and in between these spines are fitted with decorative miniature shrine-models (Manjaries) of deminishing heights. These were filled in 3 to 5 horizontal and 5 to 7 vertically upwards.

Suknasa - antefix is another feature of Bhumija temple where in a sculptured medallion with in Chaitya dormer was fitted at the base of the spine on each side. This type of decoration in front side indicate the deity as a principal derty.

Bhumija temples have been raised at Ambarnath (Distt. Dhulia) in 11th century A.D. likewise Gondeshwar temple at Sinnar (Distt. Nasik) belonging 13th century A.D. is a panchayatana temple with four subsidiary shrines. The Bhumija style of temple was prevalent in Malwa of central India.

It is to point out here that hundreds of Bhumija style of temples were raised here in 10th century A.D. The typical feature of this earliest style was group of temples Omkar Mandhata (District Nimar) is another prolific centre of Bhumija temples.

Interestingly is the fact, that this style of Malwa temple style was adopted by parts of Rajasthan, Chhattishgarh and West India region viz Gujarat.

The group of Bhumija style of temple is concern, Un (District Khargone) Omkar Mandhata and Udaipur (District Vidisha) are prominent temples of among the Bhumija mode of construction.

Nilkantheswara (Udayeshwara) temple is the grandest temple[1] of parmara architecture. This was started in 1059 and completed in 108 A.D. by Udayaditya of Parmara dynasty.

Likewise the Śiva temple at Jamli (District Dhar) Siddheswar temple at Nemawar (District Dewas), Malvai temple (Śiva Temple) of 15th century A.D. is the latest temples of style in Malwa region.

It will thus be seen that Bhumija style of Northern architecture originated in Malwas where it was patronized by the parmard rulers and had a wide vogue in the adjoining regions in the east, west and south.

It is to mention over here that a large numbers of Parmara temples in groups and isolated forms have been mentioned in preceding pages.

Parmar king Raja Bhoja (1000-1050 A.D.) was polymath a myriad minded; who combined action with contemplation theory with practice in his strenuous life of incessant battles, interspersed with compilation of some 84 known books on architecture, Astronomy and various other subjects. He is credited to have composed a famous book on architecture, the *Samrangana Sutradhara*. His conception in the temple construction was largest and colossal temple at Bhojpur in Raisen district. The temple stands on a high Jagati adjoining a ramp of composite earth which still remains to be demolished after the temple construction is over. The sanctum was conceived Navrang Mandapa but the temple is incomplete stage.

Bhojpur temple[2] is one of the grandest monuments, consecrated to a surpassing vision of the celmination of human destiny. It is also a paen of praise to the liberal, eclectic religion of greatest Parmara king. It is above all a tribute to one of the finest feats of aesthetic engineering, in which perfection of design and architectural land scaping joins hands in a happy organic communication.

---

[1] Plate 12.

[2] Plate 9.

The temple is recently conserved by the Archeological Survey of India.[1]

## Art and Architecture of Candella Period

The Çandellas, Whose origin is controversial, were the chief ruling dynasty under the imperial Gurjar Pratiharas and availed the opportunity of weak sovereignty, obviously, they attempted to establish their supremacy over their overlord and also the contemporary rulers of northern India.

During 10th-11th centuries A.D., The Çandellas of Jejka bhukti, were the paramount rulers, and they are known as great builders and connoisseurs of art and architecture.

The powerful rulers of Çandellas constructed a large number of tanks, forts, palaees and temples at Mahoba region, Kalanjar[2], Ajaigarh[3] and towns of Dudhai, Chandpur, Madanpur and Deogarh Jhansi District region. These monuments temples of these places could stand no comparision with those of the Capital town of Khajuraho in (District Chhatarpur).

Central India possesses such geographical features of which the major portion and candella territory was under the Çandellas, where a number of famous forts can still be seen in situ, like mahoba, Kalanjar and Ajaigarh forts.

During 9th to 12th century A.D. the temple art and architecture flourished to its climax with its centre at Khajuraho. Here about 85 temples of Śiva, Sakta, Vaisnava and jain cult were constructed and were prominent among the temple building activities. At present only 25 templex are surviving in good state of preservation. These temples are famous in the world for their art and architecture. Their magnificence, perfection of design and sculptural profusion make them masterpieces of architectural and sculptural art. The

---

[1] Plate 24.

[2] Fig. 3.

[3] Fig. 4.

style of architecture of these temples are nagar style and shikhara style. Raised on lofty terrace (Jagti). Normally the temples have been oriented in the east-west side. Just above jagati is adhisthan mouldings and jangha portion, well carved depicting viz. Elephants (gajthar) and Narthr. Oriel windows are meant for inlet of fresh air as well as to neutrilise the wind pressuse velocity.

## Shikhar type of temples are a like Kailash Mountain

It is to point of here that as discussed inpreceeding pages that Gupta temples are small in size and plain in decoration devoid of iconographic representation; the temples of Khajuraho[1] are huge and lofty, full of iconographic decoration, a sandhar type of construction.

The images that have been carved in temples of Khajuraho may be catagorised height wise in groups mention may be made of the various categories of Images that have been depicted are of various themes.

The first group of images that are noticed here; contain images for worship and carved round the temple in Garvhagriha, Sabha Mandapas etc. So far as their postures are concerned they are sambhanga and in sthanak position; the gods and goddesses deities. The second catagories of the images indicate the position of Parivar Devta as well as side deities (Parivardevta). These images have been carved in bold relief and fixed either inside the proper nitch or on the body of the temple on face walls.

The third categories of the images are Sursundaries, Apsaras, Naikas[2]; Such images are very large in number and depict various postures. Some where they have been depicted engaged in play with animals and birds. Such depiction was also depicted in various stupas of the Buddhist art. Prasadhanrata naika (Naika engaged in dressing) standing under the canopy of mango tree is a unique representation. The fourth categories of images that have been carved and fixed over the face walls of the temples depicting social

---

[1] Plate 10.

[2] Plate 11.

life of man, pertaining to the domestic scenes reflecting the present social life of the mankind. The fifth categories of images belong to flora, fauna, and aifauna, where in we find animals like sardul (lion with horn) which is the main representation, apart from this horses, camels, elephants and other animals have also been given due place or representation likewise parrots and other avifauna representation is a common depiction in these temples.

Interestingly is the fact that Khajuraho was one of main Kapalik centre where ratichakra mahotsave was the main function of the kapalikas, such representation have also been depicted. The erotic images depiction is an attraction for general man, as discussed above these images reflect the hold of kaul and kapalika sects here.

Representation of tantric rituals like in temples of Orissa (suntemple Konark), Puri, Bhuvenshwar are the flourishing trends of the kaul kapalisa sects in those days.

Lotus scrolls and other creepers have been vehemently represented in the temple structues full bloomed lotus and series of lotus petal representation the lotus rihizome on ceilings and pillars etc. like other temples and pillars of other dynasties.

Depiction of these environmental components in the temples testify to the act that the builders of these temples were well aware of the protection of environment by representing the elements of environment in stone art of these temples and allowing the common mass to realize the importance of environment as these temples were school of learning and worship for the common mass.

## Art and Architecture of Parmaras

Munja was a great patron of art and literature, he patronised scholars and built tanks (Munja sagar) temples at Ujjain. Mahakaleshwar temple[1] Onkareshwar Mandhata and Dharampuri paramara king Bhoja was a great

[1] Plate 18.

builder who constructed Bhojsala Saraswati temple at Dhar and Bhojpur temple and various water bodies.

Bhojpur temple stands today in its complete state like a massive carvan of the gods in the minds of a desolate rocky land scaspe. The day was when it stood on an elevation at the end of a vast sheet of water stretching continuously from Bhojpur to Bhopal (called Bhojasar).

Apart from this the remains of three cyclopean dams built successived on river Betwa near Bhojpur temple on caliasot near village Medua and on the ole Bhopal fort can still be seen.

It is to pointout here that Bhumij style of temple architecture was introduced by the paramara kings. Udaiyeshwar temple at Udaiypur is the finest specimen of temple architecture of Bhumij style. It was constructed by the paramara king Udayaditya.[1] Likewise the other temples of this style are found at un khargone district Siddheswar temple at Nemawar and group of temples at Omkareshwar Mandhata, are the temples belonging to the paramara dynasty and are based on Bhumija style of architecture.

These temples have been laviously decorated with foliage; luxuriant abundance of winding lotus rhizomes is the characteristic feature of these temples as shown in Bhojeshwar temple. Vriskhikas Naikas standing under a tree, river goddess standing below lotus canopy (sanal padma) Jain temples of this period adorned with various sculptural scenes in which Gomedh Ambika under a mango tree canopy is depiction of elements of environment.

## Art and Architecture of the Kalacuris

The art and architecture of Kalacuris flourised in

1. The Gangetic Valley
2. Narmada Valley
3. The Hilly Areas

[1] Plate 12.

## The Gengetic Valley

The river Ganga, and its tributaries like river Yamuna, Toms, Karmanasa drain the northern part which was the lower plateau of the Kalacuris kindom.

The important sites of ancient sites, monuments epigraph are Sarnath, Karnaghanta (Distt. Varanasi) Sursi (Distt. Mirzapur) Goharawa, Pabhora, Prayag (Allahabad), Alhaghat, Lalpahar (Distt. Satna).

## Narmada Valley

The valley besides providing shelters to the prehistoric and protohistoric man had also been the home of many early Indian dynasties. In this narmada basin flourished the Mauryas, the Sungas, the Guptas, the Pushayabuties, the Gurpara Pratiharas, the Rashrakutas, the Kalacuris and Paramaras etc.

This valley is a narrow strip formed by the Narmada and its tributaries like hiran etc. the southwestern part of the Kalacuri empire. Tripuri, Bheraghat, Gopalpur, Bahuriband, Bilahari, Sihora, etc. are the importance places in this valley.

## The Hilly Areas

The major part of the Kalacuri kindom was carvered by the hilly tract spread from east to west Three prominent parts of the hills may be mentioned as given below :

1. The western ranges of the Vindhyas.
2. The eastern Vindhyas and the upper Son valley
3. The south eastern ranges of the Satpura and lower Son valley

The important Kalacuri centres under western ranges of Vindhyas are, Baragaon, Chhoti Deori, Bhratola - Deori (Jabalpur Distt.) Nohta, Abhana (Distt. Damoh).

The eastern part of Vindhyas and upper Son valley posseses the following important Kalacuri centres like Gurgi, Mahsaun, Khajua, Badgaon, Rehuta, Marai, Barinath and Deotalao.

Likewise the important centres of south son are chandreh situated at the confluence of river son and its tributory banas in Sidhi Distt. Apart from these important centres, the Kalacuri centres like Sohagpur, Antara, Singhpur, Bandhorarh Amarkantaka are located in the south-eastern ranges of Satpura and lower Son valley. The monuments are mostly found along the lower course of the river son, in the east of Amarkantak escarp.

The Kalacuri architect played a significant role in the history of early medieval architecture of India. We find innovations in the temples as well as in civil architecture during the region of Kalacuri.

The door (Dvara), entrance door is an importnat part of the temple or palace. It has been invariably and elaborately described in various silpasastras.

The sculptures depicted in the temple of Kalacuri are :-

Human figures including figures of attendants, devotees etc.

Animal figures Archictureal designes.

Mythical figues like makara

Apart from the other decorations of carvings are:-

Architectural decorations

Geometrical designs

Floral designes.

Among the flora, the lead, flowers, and scrolls, creepers are invariably represented in low relief in kalcuri monuments. Apart from this vase and foliage have been vehemently depicted in the temples of Amarkantak. Mostly this motif is sculptured at the base of the dvarsakhas or at the base o the stambha to decorate likewise ghat pallavas have also been shown here.

It has renewad faith, the water nourishing the plant railing from its brim, an allegory which has produced the vase and flowers motif one of the most graceful form in the whole range of Indian architecture.

The other decorative motif design may be mentioned here which is known as rekha-karma (scroll work). It is generally used to decorate stambhas, kudyan, kudyastambhas and sometimes in dvarsakhas of the medieval temples. In few cases we find it with ratna-puspa.

In fort and palaces the garden planning was an essential feature of town planning of Indo - Aryans. The temples and salas were provided with a perfectly layed out gardens with water chanels. These were the essential components of garden planning. Certain trees and plants like peepla tulsi etc. were considered as sacred as they have the aesthetic and sanitary potentialities. The trees and plants in the well layed out garden serve the purpose of screening as well as they help in arresting the atmospheric pollutions. Looking to the above factors the garden planning formed an inseparable aspect of the palace complexes. Krida udyana Ashokavan, shalavan were a part of the palace complex.

It is more interesting to mention about a complex inside the fort which are known as Dhavalgrha- it was the residence of the king and was situated in the midst of other establishments. It was generally located in the third court. The Jahangir Mahal[1], Raja Mahal[2] at Orchha Distt. Tikamgarh palace at Datia and Agra fort are good examples of Dhavalgiha with certain modifications where chitrasala was an important component of royal palace complex. The description of chitrasalas are found in various sanskrit texts like the Ramayana. An Antahpur chitrasala is nicely described in Bhavabhuti in his Uttara Ram charita such chitrasala are found in the palaces like Orchha, Datia, Narwar, Gohad, Vijai Raghogarh; Dhar, Mandu. The other establishments which is important from the point of view of enivronments are Grihodyana (the garden of the palace), it was known as bhavanodyana

[1] Plate 21.

[2] Plate 22.

or manderodyan which was adorned with leafy and flowery trees; consisting of garden pavilions. The lotus ponds are the complex of the garden with kirdaparvataka artificially raised mound for pleasure resort of the kings and the queens.

Grihodirghika the artificially made flowing canal for discharging fountains and water ponds. In chitrasala paintings of flora fauna avifauna, sun, moon, hills etc. are depicted the main elements of environment which have been represented in the various fort and palaces in India.

Interestingly enough that during the reign of Kalauri king Raja Prithvideo I (1069-1095 A.D.) governed by a branch of Ratanpur Kalauri constructed a temple known as Bhorandeo temple.[1] The temple is situated in the Mekhala range of hills about 18km. north west of present district town kawardha.

This temple is known as Khajuraho of Chhattisgarh. The temple was constructed in 11th century A.D. It is oriented in eastern disection and is an unique Nagar style of temple, construction with out an ambulatory passase (A Nrandhar temple).

The temple consist of three entrance gates North, south & front east side. The temple consists of a Jagati (Adhisthan) except in sanctum In plan is identical to the temples of Khajaraho and contain a square garbhagirh (sanctum) vestibule (Antarala), Mandapa (Hall) and two side ardha mandapas and front portico.

The temple is well carvel with images of gods and goddesses are interspersed with those of secular Naikas. Śiva is found in peaceful and voilent poses and the Ardha narishwara image illustrate the symphony of the Indian principle of purusha prakati, the chinese yin-yang, the tibetian yab-yum. Warlike scenes, scenes vibrant with music and dance, carnal and festive activites have been offset by images lost in calm contemplation, looking deep inside themselves. The mithuna images may be baffling in sexual pyrotechnics, but they are meant not to deflct the seeker from askesin but to

[1] Plate 23.

test his faith and to induce him to enter the sanctum sanctorum where peace and silence reign. Enjoyment here is a gate way to renunciation. External physical activity is a prelude to the inner spiritual yearning and effort.

## Temple of Dwaraka

Every year thousands of pilgrims visit the holy town of Dwarka to pay homage to lord Krishna at the temple of Dwarakadhish.[1] According to sabha parva of Mahabharat Krishna accompanied by his Yadav followers migrated to Dwarka to escape Jarasandha's attack on Mathura.

The Yadavas ledby Srikrishna sought shelter on the west coast where the town kusasthali built by kakadmin Raivata, a Yadava, once stood. Ṛgveda refers to the yadus in Anarta country that is Gujarat which was named after Anarta, the son of Monu. Kakudmin Raivata was one of the descendants of Anarta. From the statements made in the sabha parva impregnable forts were built to make the town inhabitable.

Dwarka's submerged structures are being explored and excavated by scientists. The present temple of Dwarka is a lofty magnificent temple resembling northern style of sikhara.

### Monuments of Orissa

The orissan temple style of construction was centered at Bhubneshwar, Puri and Konark all in Puri District. Orissa (Ancient Kalinga) extend from the boarder District of Bihar and Bengal to Ganjam in Andhra Pradesh.

The temple architecture of Orissa is a distinctive regional style and traditional architectural nomenclature or the terms for the components were used in oriya version.

Apparently seventh century A.D. May be regarded as the origin of earliest temple construction in Orissa Bhubneshwar group of temples can

---

[1] Plate 19.

be placed as the culmination of temple construction during thirteen century A.D. when the Sun temple at Konark was constructed.

In the core of this ancient city Bhubneshwar clusters of densely carved, beehive shaped temples testify to Orissas later days of glory between 7th to 15th centuries when oriyan Hindu culture was at its culmination. During that time Bhubneshwar was Known as Ekamsarshetra and was one of the five religious centers in Orissa.

About seven hundred temples were raised around the sacred Bindusagar lake alone, of which about hundreds are survived even after human vandlism during 16th century A.D. Noteworthy is feature of sun temple, dedicate to sun god was built here at Konark in 13th C.A.D. is one of the flnest in India.

Likewise another most notable of the temples is the Lingraj temple[1] built during 11th century A.D., dedicated to lord siva. prior to the construction of Lingraj temple, Mukteshwar temple was built in 10th C.A.D. decorated with highly intricate and eleborate stone carvings.

The orissan temples broadly pertain to three orders, locally known as

Rekha - deul

Pidha - deul

Khakhara - deul

The sanctum with its curvilinear shikhara (rekha) is called rekha-deul and the mandapa (Jagmohana) with its pyramidical roof of pidhas (tiers) is known as pidha deul.

In a typical Orissan temple, the latter two form the component parts of a single architectural scheme.

The later orissan temples, two more mandapas were added in front elevation, they are known as Nata mandapas (dancing hall) and Bhoga mandapa (hall of offerings) in the same axis.

---

[1] Plate 30.

Likewise the temples of the third order, viz, Khakhara deul are rare.

The noteworthy feature of these temple is that they possess an of long plan and a wagon - vault roof, which a familiar shape in south India, probably derived from the early chaitya halls later on a shape known as khakhara mundi was commonly used as decorative architectural feature.

The course of evolution in Orissa is towards a greater elaboration of the plan and elevation and increasing sophistication of ornaments.

The early examples of temple construction resemble with a modest size and squat sikhara and showing native sculptures and ornaments, mature into elaborate structures of a towering height, embellished with exuberant iconographic, lataballaries depiction with fine carving in low and high relief's.

The size of the sanctum and height sikhara is 1:3 in ratio, at the initial stage of development of temple style, as seen in the parashurameshwara temples decorated with Śiva, Harihara Lakulisḥa Surya, Agni, Yama, Varuna, Ganga and Yamina and sapta inatrieas flanked by virbhadra and Ganesh respectively.

The ratio becomes into 1:7 in the latest construction of temple are in seen temple at konark. Another temple viz vaital deul among the earliest group is Labiously decorated than Parashurameshwar, which have attained a maturity and its relief images are more expressive and dynamic. This temple is datable to the close of 8th century A.D.

The Shishiseshwara and Markandeveshwara temple closed resemble the vaital deul. One of the finest example of Orissan temple architecture is Mukteshwar temple which is regarded as a gem of temple architecture, marks a transition between the earlier and the later groups of temple in Bhubneswar. Siddheshwar has a panch-rath sanctum and resmbles with that of Kedareshwara temple.

The Lingraj temple belonging circa 11th century A.D. is the grandest and loftiest temple, marking culmination of the temple architecture of

Bhubneshwar. It may be noted in the present context that the culmination of temple architecture style was reached in the sun temple at Konark[1] marks the grandest achievement of the artistic and architectural genius of Orissa and pinnacle of Kalinga architecture.

The magnificent temple is dedicated to Surya, the "Sun god", who is shown riding the heavens in a magnificent Chariot of stones with twelve pairs of great stone wheels which represent the cycle of the Sun.[2] Seven galloping horses draw the Chariot along its sacred pathways in the sky. Stone musicians celebrate the Sun god's procession from atop a thigh parapet, and below, the entire gamut of life is represented.

The Sun temple not only marks the final fulfillment of Orissan architecture, but is one of the sublimest monument of India.

## Southern Region

### The Later Chalukyan Temples

In preceding pages a detailed account of Early Chalukyan temples have been discussed. In the present context the temple architecture under Hoysalas of Mysore belonging to circa 12th and 13th Century A.D. is the main study of distinctive style of temple architecture of the dynasty.

This temple architecture is altogether being influenced by the Northern as well as southern style of temple architecture a separate distinctive style in which the greenish chloritic schist was vehemently used in the construction of monuments.

The typical Hoysala temple is built on high polygonal Jagati conforming in shape to the main structure. It is because the Jagati is being used for processional passage.

---

[1] Plate 31 (A).

[2] Plate 31 (B).

The main structure being the simplest unit consisting of a Sanctum (Garbha-grih), a vestibule and a pillared sabha mandapa. Which is attached infront by a open pillared pavilion.

In plan the temple is in stellate shape which is another unique feature of the temple of Hoyasala period likewise the sikhara is stellate on plan and sizes above the projecting cornice in diminishing horizontal tiers crowned by a low paracal shaped finial. It is to pointout here that lavious use of images at appropriate places in the temple have been fixed in the temple is the indication surprising that the ivory carvers or Jewelles have completed this task of carving in the temple structure and not by the architects.

The following temples have been built up at halibid in District hassan of Mysore.

The Chenna-kesha temple 1140-1170 A.D. and the Hoysaleshwar temple in 1150 A.D.

These temple depict the ingenious plastic ornamentation. Mark of the maturity of construction in the style of temple architecture. The most typical and complete example of fully evolved Hoysala style is the Keshava temple at Somnathpur[1] and asigned a period of construction in the year 1268 A.D.

It is an architectural gem of Hoyasalla style of temple architecture notablefor its balanced composition and faultless proportions.

As regards the later (or western) Chalukyan architecture, with Kalyanas their capital, the original traditions were continued with a gradual introduction of significant modifications of essentially southern types of vimana.

It is to point out here that the sandstone as building material was in vogue as seen in the temples like Navalinga group and slightly later Kaleshwara temple at Kukkanur near Gudag (Distt. Dharwar) would perhaps mark the end of sand stone tradition of eastern Chalukyas adopted the chloritic schist.

---

[1] Plate 36.

Some of the excellent example of temples viz Kasi-vishveswar temple at Ittagi mark the area as its zenith under western Chalukyas.

On the other hand the temple at Hanankonda (Distt. Warangal) called thousand pillared temple is a tradition from the late Chalukyan to the Kakatiya temples of this region. It was built in 12th century A.D. and is dedicated to Śiva, Vishnu and Surya.

The reined temple with in the Fort Warangal is a testimony for the elaborate tornas. The group of temples at palam (District Warangal) is a typical Kakatiya monuments built in the begining of 13th century A.D., stands on a high Jagati and is enclosed by a massive wall.

The Nandi mandapa is infront, while the main viman is square plan from the base to the sikhara, the side offset are in five bays, while the central offset as the most projecting facet and containing a three-tiered replica in miniature of the main vimana. The griva is of the same width as the square and the domical Sikhara. The entire superstructure is built in brick work in lime mortar.

During the reign o Pallava king parmesivra verman in the last quarter of seventh century A.D., a distinctive feature of the temple construction in stone masony was started. It was essentially an experimental point of view. The following temple of Pallavas were raised during the reign of Pallava kings Parmesvara varman, Rajasimha, Mahendra varman, Nandivarman pallavamalla,

Veagirisvara at Tirukkalukkunsam.

Apsidul temple at Kuram

Shore temple at Mahabalipuram[1]

Kshtriyasimhesvara temple

Talagirisvara temple at Pannamalai

Kailasanatha temple complex at Kanchi

[1] Plate 32.

Vikuntha - Perumal temple at Kanchi

Mukanda - Nayanar temple at Mahbalipuram

Muktesvara, Matangesvara, Aira Vatesvara, Valisvara, Iravatesvara and Piracatanesvara all at Kanchi, built mainly of sand stone, veneered with granite slabs.

The early pandyas followed the rock cut architecture viz. Single carved out monolithic vimanas at Kalugumalai.

It is to point out here that the pandayas of south continued the architectural work akin to that of the pallavas but with a slight admixture of Chalukyan traits.

The S'via temples at Triruvalisvaram and korkai (Distt. Tirunelveli). However, Tiruvalis varam viman was constructed in (900-50A.D.) white Akkasalai temple at korkai is much plainer in design of a later date.

During the half of ninth century the Pallavas and Pandyas were uprooted by the imperial cholas of Thanjavur and succeeded to the hegmony in the south.

This period may be noted as the culmination of temple architecture, when a large number of earlier temples of brick- and timber were renovated in stone and more were built.

A typical Early Chola temple-unit to Sundaresvara at Tirukattalai (Thiruchhirappali Distt.). The temple unit was built in stone only. Similar to the above temple is the Nagesvara temple at Kumbarkonam (Distt. Thanjavur). The Korasiganatha temple at Srinivasanaalur (Distt. Thiruchirapalli) is an elegant example of the time of Parantaka I (907-55 A.D.) The temple was built in brick structure.

Among the temple construction by Chollas, the Brihadesvara temple callted Rajarajesvara, built by Rajaraja 1 (985-1014 A.D.) and is gracious, and the most ambitious under taking of temple architecture of Tamil.[1] The

[1] Archaeological Remains Monuments & Museum, Part II - P. 232.

construction of the temple Begun in 1003 A.D. and completed in 1010 A.D. The chola paintings form a fine gallery of great artistic inset and iconographic interest.

Likewise a good number of temples complex were built on either bank side of the Kaveri river in (Thirachhanapalli Distt.) by the Irukkuvel chiefs, who were the feudotories of cholla dynesty. The gopura and the vimanas carry on their walls and niches some of the finest early Chola sculptures.

Likewise the Vijay Nagar empire which encompassed the whole of the peninsula in 14th C.A.D. when they came into power, continued the traditions of Chalukyas, later Cholas and Pandyas.

The northern temples in deccon and Andhra Region was an inspiration of Chalukyas.

Among the many large Vijaynaragra temples are at Hampi such as Pampapati and Virupaksha[1], worth mention over here.

## Features of Southern Temples

The southern temples with their characteristic tiered viman shrines, major and minor, their axial and peripherial manadapa adjuncts, which are flat-roofed halls and the towering gopura[2] entrances form a distinct class by theselves as against the Northern prusada temples with their curvilinear superstructure, the crowing amalaka and mandapas with rising tiered roofs. That the vimana form in its various plan and elevations built of brick and timbe had already been developed in the south before the 7th century A.D.

South Indian temple, architecture, sculpture and iconography may be said to have had a great share in this. Infact it may be said that many of the greatest achievements in the fields of religion, art and architecture are to be found in regions beyond the cradle centres of the great religions in

---

[1] Plate 33.

[2] Plate 37.

south India- as at Thanjaar and madurai, and in other lands as in Java and cambodia.[1]

# Islamic Monuments of India

## Prominent traits of Indo-Islamic architecture

The muslim invasion and conquest of India, made a distinctive impact on the indigenous expressions of life and culture.

The above effect resulted a new style in the art and architecture. This style incorporated not nobly certain new modes and principles of construction but reflected also the religious and social needs of adherents of Islam.

It is to note that the construction under the Brahmanical, Buddhist or Jain construction, spaces were spanned either by beams or by courses of bricks or stone laid in corbel, so that open space was gradually reduced to a size which could be covered with the single slab.

Indus valley civilization provides us the information about evidence of true arch, it is the muslims who are believed to have brought with them the principle of building a true arch, so that courses of bricks or stones could be laid as voussoirs to reproduce a curve and thus span the space between columns or walls.

Infact it may be said that muslims reintroduce the building of arch firmly implanted on the soil.

This resulted that flat lintels or corbelled ceilings were replaced by arches or vaults, and pyramidal roof (Pidha) or spire (Sikhara) by dome. The squinehes were added in the open spaces so that a base with many sides, usually sixteen, could be obtained to raise a circular drum for the dome. A sunshade or balcony was laid on cantilever brackets fixed into and projecting from the walls, which introduced the Chhajja (eaves or sunshade). Brackets with richly carved pendentives, described as stalactite pendentives.

[1] Shrinivasan. K.R. - Temples of South India- P. 5.

Kiosks (Chhattries), tall towers (Minars) and half domed double portals are some of the other distinguishing features of Indo-Islamic architecture.

The difference between the layout of a temple and a mosque is explained by the essential difference between the Hindu and forms of worship and prayer.

A cella to house the image of the deity (Garbha-griha), and often small halls in front for the worshipers (Mandapa) were regarded adequate for simple Hindu temple. But the Islamic form of warship, with its emphasis on congregational prayer, requires a spacious court yard (Sihn) with a large prayer hall (liwan) at its western end. In the rear wall of the prayer hall the centre is occupied by a recess or alcove, called Mihrab, and indicates the direction of the prayer (qibla).

A pulpit (mimbar) to its right is meant for the Imam who leads the prayer. A tower or minaret, originally intended for the muezzin to call the faithful to the prayer, later assumed a mere architectural character.

A gallery or compartment is sometimes screened off in a corner of prayer hall or in other parts to accommodate the ladies who observed purdah. The main entrance to a mosque is on the east, and the sides are enclosed by cloisters (liwans). A tank is provided for ablutions usually in the courtyard of a mosque.[1]

The practice of the burial of the dead, as distinct from the cremation practised by the Hindus, introduced the tomb. A domed chamber (hujra) with a cenotaph (Zarih) in its centre, a mihrab in the western wall, and the real grave (Qabr) in an underground chamber (Maqbara) constitute the esential elements of a tomb. In larger and more complex tombs, there is also a mosque, and in later tombs a well planned garden. The entrance to the mortuary-chamber is usually from the south.

The mode, theme or motifs of ornamentation employed in the Islamic buildings also made a departure from earlier Hindu Vogues. The indigeneous

---

[1] Fig. 7.

ornamentation is largely naturalistic, delineating with a conspicuous zest human and animan forms and the luxuriant vegetation-life, characteristics of a tropical country.

Among the Muslims, the representation of living beings was forbidden by scriptural injuction, and so they took recourse to execution of geometrical and arabesque patterns, of ornamental writing and a floral representation of plant and floral life, reflecting in its scantiness the nature of the country where Islam was born. Lucidity and simplicity of expression, economic use of material and orderly arrangement Characterize the Islamic art, as distinct from the exuberance, richness and exaggeration of Hindu art. The ornamental design in Islamic building were carved on stone in low relief, cut on plaster, gilded, painted or inlayed.

Muslim ornamentation even on stone or other base in effect is not much different from. embroidery. striking colour effect was often obtained by encaustic enamel on tiles.

Lime was known earlier in India but its use was limited, mud being used for brick work while large blocks of stone were generally laid dry and secured with each other by means of iron clamps. The Muslim, on the other hand made an extensive use of lime, which served not nearly as a binding medium, but also as plaster and a base for incised decoration and encaustic enamel work.

Indo-Islamic architecture falls under three broad phases. The monuments erected by or under the patronage of the Delhi sultanat belong to the first phase.

Contemporaneously at least in part, monument were also coming up in the different provinces, which were originally ruled by governors appointed by sultans, but which soon declared themselves independent.

These exhibit a diversified but distinctive phase. To the third phase belong the construction of the mughals, who brought India again under an almost united suzerainty.

The monuments in Delhi belong to the first and third class, while among important monuments of the first class there exist only two outside Delhi- the Arhai-Din-ka-Jhoppra at Ajmer and the Jami - Musjid at Bari khatu, district Nagpur - Delhi and Agra share between them selves the largest number of monuments erected by or associated with the Mughal rulers.

Prior to the advent of Mughals in India, Qutbud-din Aibak was the powerful ruler in Delhi, fire dynasties raised a large number of monuments which made possible for the development of Islamic architecture in India and its further growth in this activity was enhanced later by the mighty power of Muaghals.

The following dynasties of Sultans is responsible for growing and development of art and architecture of during the period they ruled.

| | | |
|---|---|---|
| 1. | Slave or Mamtuk dynasty | |
| | Including Balban and his successors | 1206-1290 A.D. |
| 2. | Khalji dynasty | 1290-1321 A.D. |
| 3. | Tughluq dynasty | 1321-1414 A.D. |
| 4. | Sayyid dynasty | 1414-1444 A.D. |
| 5. | Lodi dynasty | 1444-1526 A.D. |

Qutbud-din-Aibak is responsible for the early construction activity. Since it was not possible for them to follow the norms of the building activities as there was a shortage of skilled workers in India to follow the rules of there own homeland.

In this context, it is to point out here that many of the monuments were built with the architectural members well decorated and carved from the demolished Hindu temples and temples which were demolished by him. Qutb Minar was raised as a stone lower of victory the tallest stone tower of

India.[1] Close to the Qutb Minar, he constructed a Masque by using the well carved, decorated stone members from the demolished temples.

The earliest existing monumental Muslim tomb was built likewise with the stone members of demolished temples in Distt. Kutch.

Alaud-Din Khalji is well known for his architectural ambitions and achievements. The main characteristic features of Khalji buildings is decorating the arch with "lotus bud" bring on the underside of the arch.

The employment of true arch pointed horse-shoe, broad dome, recessed arches under the squinches, perforated Jali windows, decorative mouldings arabasque low relief, inscriptional bands and use of red sand stone and use of marble are some of the architectural features of Khalji architecture.

Among the eleven rulers of Tughluq dynasty three of them were interested in architecture and each added a new capital city in Delhi.

The red sand stone was vehemently employed in the architecture of Tughluq dynasty. Their building are distinguished by plain and austre surfaces of grey stone. Cross -vaults over large halls, battered wall and bations on the quoins, four-centered arches, and lintels above the openings.

So far as decorative features of this dynasty it pertains inscribed boarders and medallions in spandrels where use of stucco- plaster was the main designs.

It is to note that like the Sultanate dynasty discussed in the preceding pages the Sayyid dynasty was no patronization of arts and building activities like construction of palaces, and mosques it. Only tombs were raised at appropriate places. Like Mohammad Shahs tomb in the Lodi-garden. It is octagonal in plane, consisting of raised drum and so its height of the structure.

It looks much more impressive than the tomb o Mubarak Shah. So far as the building activities during Lodi dynasty, It may be taken into account

[1] Plate 25.

that during the power of Sikandar and Ibrahim, there was no impetus for raising new monuments, excepts some of the tombs in the two styles that had come into vogue during sayyid dynasty.

Two mosques built in Delhi during the rule of the Lodis deserve mention over here, they were equipped with certain features which developed into important characteristics in the Mughal period.

Sultan's of Malwa politically were very strong and constructed large number of monuments as Mandu which displays a great variety of styles of the art and architecture at one place.

It is interesting to note that constructions of Sultans of Mandu generally consists of small stones of basalt used in superstructure and domes of the Mosques, Tombs and Kiosks in coursed and rubble masonry in Lime Mortar and disguising a Lukhuri brick masonry in concentric bricks of domes.

Likewise, in the front facades of Mosque, Tombs, Lameta stone, ashlar masonry with blocks of stones have labilously been used.[1]

Similarly the ceilings and soffits and arches were veneered by the slabs of lameta stones in lime mortar. While marble was freely used along with other colours black yellow with semiprecious stones, jesper, agate and cornelion inside the interiors, facades emphasing in a most, artistic manner their animated character.

One of distingusing features of the architecture of mosques of Mandu is the absence of Minars.

Noteworthy is the fact that defferent varieties of arches, trabeat, equilateral, depresed, gothic four centred and ogee and domes like hemispherical, segmental, pyramidal are seen at one place.

---

[1] Dr. Singh A.P.- Monuments of Mandu P. 165-66.

**Northern Group**

1. The Jami Masijed
2. Tomb of Hoshang Shah
3. Ashasfi Mahal
4. Tomb of Mahmud Khalji
5. Taveli Mahal
6. Jahaj Mahal
7. Hindola Mahal
8. Champa Baoli.
9. The Royal Enclave
10. Dilwar Khan's Mosque
11. Nahar Jharokha
12. Hathi Pol
13. Ujali and Andheri Baoli
14. Gada-Shah Shop and Palace
15. Chisti Khan's Palace

**Southern Group**

1. Buz Bahadur's Palace
2. Rupmatis Pavilion
3. Rewa Kund Apartments

**Eastern Group**

1. Adhar Gumbaj
2. Jali Mahal
3. Dai ka Mahal
4. Dai ki Chooti Bahen ka Mahal
5. Carvan Sarai
6. Malik Mugheth's Mosque
7. Darya Khan's Tomb
8. Hathi Mahal
9. Lal Bungalow

**Western Group**

1. Chhappan Mahal
2. Ek Khamba
3. Nil- Kanth.

# Mughal Region

Babur was a man of culture and exceptional aesthetic taste. He is credited to have laid two gardens, One at Agra and the other at Panipat. owing to lack of skilled artisans' and stone carvers he was not impressed with their working and hence could not built any important monument except Kabulbagh mosque at Panipat and another, Jama-Masjid at Sambhal and one at Ayodhya, which finds mention in Babar nama (his memoirs).

In the early days of his occupation of the Mughal thrown, he remained in struggle with Sher-Shah-Suri and also being addict of drugs, he under these circumstances could not cultivate the activities of art and architecture at Delhi. His first contribution in this activity was completing the parts of Purana- Quila which Sher-Shah-Suri could not complete. He also completd Jamali-Kamali-Masjid at Mehrauli which Babur couldnot complete during his region. This mosque has an important place in the evolution of Mughal-mosque.

After the death of Humayun, his senior widow, Bega Begum known as Haji Begum completed his tomb after ten years of his demise[1], the first distinct example of the proper Mughal style which inspired by persion architecture.

Interestingly is the fact that the Tomb of Humayun is a synthesis of Persian architecture and Indian traditions. with its arched alcoves, Corridors and high double dome, and the latter by kiosks, imparting it a pyramidal profile and by such features as use of beam and lintel in dalans. As mentioned above that first tomb of Sikandar Lodi, the first garden tomb to be built in India. It is Humayuns tomb which set up a new vogue, the crowning achievement of which is the Taj-Mahal[2] at Agra by Emperor Shahjahan.

There is also a some what common human by a devoted wife for her husband and the other by an equally or more devoted husband for his wife.

---

[1] Plate 27.

[2] Plate 29.

Akbar was the eldest son of Humayan, he ascended the throna at the age of thirteen years. He was keenly interested in art and architecture. The Mughal style of painting developed under guidance, as a result of fusion of Hindu and Persian techniques.

His architecture is characterized equally by happy blending of the indigenous and Islamic modes of construction and ornamentation with an exception of Humayun tomb.[1]

Akbar was the first Emperor, who initiated Mughal style of architecture, gave it a character of its own for the first time.

Agra was the capital seat of Emperpor Akbar, where he built his famous fort and raised a new township at Fatehpur- Sikri, His tomb at Sikandara also lies on the out Skirts of Agra. Akbar raised certain Mughal buildings of Delhi, viz Adham Khan's tomb at Mehrauli built in 1562 A.D. is octagonal and is in the Lodi style, with the deference, that it lacks the usual Chhajja. Maham Anga a wet-nurse of Akbar, herself built in 1561-62 Khairal-Manazil Masjid infront of Purana-Quila. Another tomb of Ataga khan was raised in 1566-67 in Nizamuddin is a square chamber masle of red sand stone.

Jahangir occupied the Mughal throne in 1605 A.D. after the death of Akbar. He was a pleasure loving and fond of natural beauty devoid of an art and architecture. Miniature paintings attracted him most and infact, the credit goes to him for the development of Mughal painting in India. The tomb of his father and father in law are two major monuments at Agra in which he took interest. Towards the later part of his reign certain monuments were also raised in Delhi.

Another Mughal architectural monument known as Safdar-jang tomb[2] is similar to Humayun's tomb in basic design, Infact this tomb is of Mirza Muqim Abul-Masnsur Khan, viceroy of oudh under Muhammadshah (1719-48) and later on prime Ministers under Ahmad Shah (1748-54).

---

[1] Plate 27.

[2] Plate 28.

At Srinagar in Kashmir, Nurjahan built the Patthar- Masjid, while Jahangir engaged himself in arranging the gardens. He died in 1627 A.D. and his tomb at Shahdra near Lahore was built later by his devoted Queen.

After the death of Jahangir in 1662. Shahjahan ascended the throne. Though Shajahan inherited the artistic taste of his father, but he facinated towards the architecture of the monument and gratified him and remained his life long passion.

Prior to the mughal period other of dynasties used sand stone and even up to Mughal Emperor, Jahangir, the red sand stone was used as building material.

Shahjahan preferred marble to other stones. His buildings are characterized by a form and feeling of feminity, sensuousness and delicateness, as distnict from the study, robust and relatively plain appearance of construction of Akbar.

Ornamentation therefore plays a dominant role in his buildings. Delicate carvings in marble were given due place in the monuments built by Shahjahan, almost like filigree and to fine in lay and painting. The arch became foliated and the dome received a persian form bulbus in outline and constricted at the neck. The pillars are raised with shafts resting on foliated bases and crowned by involutes bracket capitals.

Shahjahan preplanned the fort at lahore and Agra and added several monuments with in them, in the latter he even demolished some buildings of sand stone and replaced them with marble the Khas-mahal, Machchi-Bhavan (A fish palace) Diwan-I-Aam Diwan-I-khas and Motimasjid are some of the buildings erected by him in that fort.

They are all in marble displaying tapering shafts, engrailed arches and beautiful relief and inlay work in coloured stones.

Shahjahan built his Jami-Masjid in Delhi and a Masjid of the same name at Agra in honour of his Daughter Jahanara. It is smaller in size of Masjid at Delhi.

The Culmination of Mughal architectural achievements, however is Taj-Mahal[1] tomb of his beloved wife Arjmand Banu Begum, entitled Mumtaz Mahal.

The Taj mahal is the culmination of the conception of a garden-tomb which had a modest beginning in Sikandar Lodi's tomb but had advanced to mature stage in Humayan's tomb both at Delhi.

The Taj is noted for its graceful proportions and satisfying balace between the claims of architecture and ornamentation.

The profuse use of semiprecious and multi coloured stones in its floral and arabesque pattern, fine boarders, inscriptions in black marble, low relief carvings delicate traceries and trellis work, all executed in or against the background of white marble lend a unique chorm to this word famous monument.

His famous fort Lal Qila[2] is different from that of Agra fort and is better planned. It is irregular in plan with octagonal shape. with two long side on the east west flanked by two main gates, one on the west and the other on the south, called Lahori and Delhi Gates respectively made of red sand stone, marble has been used in large in the palaces erected within fort. Shahjahan built Jama - Masjid at Delhi, the lagest Mosque in India.

Likewise in Deccan at Bijapur a large number monuments were built by the dynasties ruling at Bijapur and Golkunda which were cultural in herietors of Bahmani dynasty and developed their own distinct styles of architecture. At Bijapur Jami-masjid[3] and Golgumbad[4] are splendid monuments of the dynasty.

---

[1] Plate 29.

[2] Plate 26.

[3] Fig. 7.

[4] Plate 40.

# Secular Monuments

## Other Forts and Palaces

In preceding pages we have discussed in brief about some important forts and fortification of India in different periods of history of India in general and Madhya Pradesh in particular.

It is clear, however that certain features which characterize the Islamic construction were not confined merely to Muslim forts, Palaces, Mosques and Tombs but were also incorporated by the Hindu, who also made use of some of the indigenous feature and planned their buildings to suit their customs and ways of living.[1]

Rajasthan, central India and parts of South India are rich in such palaces. Man-Mandir in the fort of Gwalior is the earliest palace, among the pre-Mughal Hindu palaces.

It is situated as it on a cliff , built by Raja Man Singh Tomar (1406-1516 A.D.) The long facade of the fort broken by circular towers at regular intervals, crowned with domed cuploas.[2]

Mughal Emperor Babur, during his visit to Gwalior fort he was impressed only by this one among the Hindu palaces and Akbar no doubt borrowed some of the architectural features from it.

The palaces built during the Mughal period may be different from each other in plan but they have certain common architectural features, viz. balconies supported on carved brackets, pillared kiosks crowned by domes, arcades of sunk arches, foliated arches, latticed screens, curved Bangal Caves and flat domes rising from a rectangular base.

---

[1] Fort and fortification of p. 70 - 77. A.P. Singh.

[2] Plate 14.

Among the important palace where magnificent palaces are situated are Amber, Jaipur, Bikaner, Jodhpur, Udaipur, Jaisalmer[1], Orchha[2] and Datia.

In south India, the Islamic principles of construction penetrated into the Hindu palace much more gradually. At Hampi the capital of Vijaynagara Kingdome about 1575 A.D. was built a double storey parition called the "Lotus-Mahal" on a square plan with double recesses at corners.

[1] Plate 35.

[2] Plate 21, 22.

Chapter 5

# EPILOGUE

The foregoing pages give a detailed account of the monuments located at various regions of India viz. North and Central India, south India East and West India.

Madhya Pradesh (Central India) be situated in the very of India, a natures parodies, endowed with extensive forest resources, rich and fertile soil, perennial rivers, varied and wide flora and fauna and vast expanse of cultivable area has been a meeting ground of different cultures since the earliest times. the two stone ages industries of the North and the peninsular India are available, here. It has the largest group of prehistoric painted rock-shelters (Bhimbetka), the world heritage monument, and it is here Besanagar (Distt Vidisha) that the contemporaneity of chalcolithic and painted grey ware cultures has been noticed for the first time.

Many aspects of Indian art and architecture appear to have originated and flourished in this part of the country.

The earliest temple (4th - 3rd century B.C.) in its fully developed form (Besanagar elliptical temple).

During early historic period the cultural activities of Maurya and Sunga, satavahana period reached to the climax in the Buddhist art and architecture which gained popularity all over the Buddhist world. Maximum number of temples of the Gupta period in various stages of development. (Udaigiri, Sanchi, Tigowa, Bhumra, Nachna Nagod etc.) the most flourishing centres of art and iconography.

Elaborately carved and elegantly spired temples of the Aryan style (Khajuraho, Udaipur, Un, Bhorandeo) and a temple displaying the features of the Aryan and Dravadian style (Teli-ka Mandir) are some of the notable contributions of the region of central India.

Because of its strategic position Madhya Pradesh has all the varieties of forts including the largest fort of the world (Mandu) and most impregnable and invincible forts like Gwalior, Narwar, Raisen and Asirgarh.

No other state has yielded so many large-sized Yaksha sculptures of Muryan and Sunga period as Madhya Pradesh. The indigenous art of Bharhut and Sanchi embellished with the cosmic expressions and representing the specimen of the Buddhist art in India. The symbolic reorientations of Ganga and Yamuna in human form and maiden depictions of Puranic themes became a source of inspiration for future artist of India.

With the increase and development of these cultural centres the architecture and oceanography roused to its high esteem. Bagh caves at Bagh (District Dhar) are superve in Mural art of Gupta period and later Gupta period and alike these of Ajanta paintings at Ajanta caves in Maharashtra.

The early medieval period the dynastics like Çandellas, Kalacuries hailed over this terretory the famous temples of Khajuraho are superve and reached to the culmination of temple architecture in the patronage of Candella dynasty.

Likewise the Kalacuri temples at Tripuri Gurgi, Janjgir, Ratanpur are the famous centres of art and architecture.

Bhumija style of temples architecture was introduced by the paramaras of Malwa. Many paramara temples were raised at Ujjain, Omkareshwar-Mandhata, Dhar, Dharampuri, Udaipur (Distt. Vidisha) Siddheswar temple at Nemavar (Dewas), and a group of temples at Un (District Khargon.) are some of the great specimen of art and architecture which influence the other contemporary dynasties in the central India. These monuments display a vision of Harmony in the particular region where they flourish.

While the Gupta temples was being built in central and North India. The early Chalukyan sites a Aihole, Badami, Mahakutkeshwar and Pattadkal are noteworthy monuments of this region.

Likewise the temple of central India and Rajasthan dating from 8th and 9th century A.D., have certain common features,. belonging to pratihara period. The Rock-cut temple complex at Masrur (District Kangra) belonging to 8th-9th century is also notable monuments of Considerable artistic and architectural significance.

In the above context of Solanki temples of Gujarat region also display individual features of temple architecture, Sun temple at Modera is good example marks the greatest achievement of Solanki Style.

The temples at Bandogarh (District Shahdol in Madhya Pradesh), belonging to pratihara genre, do reveal certain regional Kalacuri traits.

The last Kalacuri temple to be noticed in Chausatha Yogini temple at Bheraghat are require special mention. The area between the river Tapti on the North and upper branch of Krishna on the south flourished an individual style of Narthern architecture.

The development of the North Indian temple architecture in well illustrated by the temples in stone of the Orissa style, concentrated at Bhubneshwar, Puri and Konark. Lingraj temple and Sun temple at Konark are the specimen superve in Orissan art and architecture.

Hoysala temple, a distinctive type of temple architecture, chiefly raised by greenish chlorite schist is a specific representation among the temple architecture. The most typical and complete example of fully evolved Hoysalla style is the Keshavdeo temple at Somanathpur, an architectural gem.

South Indian temple architecture, sculpture and iconography may be said to have had a great share with their characteristic tired viman shrines. It may be said. That many of the greatest achievements in the fields of religion, art and architecture are to be found in religious beyond the cradle centres of the great religions in South India as at Thanjavar and Madurai and in other lands as in Java and Combodia.

Islamic monuments of India representation of mode, theme or motifs of ornamentation, that was employed here. These monuments also made a departure from earlier Hindu Vogues.

The indigeneous ornamentation is largely naturalistic, delineating with a conspicuous zest, human and animal forms and the luxuriant vegetation life, characteristic of a tropical country.

Among the Muslims the representation of living being was forbidden by scriptural injuction, and so they took recourse to execution of geometrical and arabesque patterns, of ornamental writing and a floral representation of plant and floral life, reflecting in its scantiness the nature of the country where Islam was born.

Lucidity and simplicity of expression, economic use of material and orderly arrangement characterize the Islamic art, distinct from the exuberance, richness and exaggeration of Hindu art. The ornamental designs in Islamic buildings were carved on stone in low relief, cut on plaster, gilded, painted or inlayed.

Muslim ornamentation even on stone or other base in not different from embroidery. Striking colour effect was often obtained by encaustic enamel on tiles.

Lime was known earlier in India, but its use was limited, mud being used for brick work, while large blocks of stone were generally dry by percussion method and secured with each other by means of iron clamps.

The Muslim, on the other hand made an extensive use of lime, which served not mearly as a binding medium, but also as plaster and a base for incised decoration and encaustic enemel work.

# SELECT BIBLIOGRAPHY


**Sanskrit Text**

Rg-Veda - F. Max Mullar Poona 1890-92.

Atharva-Veda - S.P. Pandit Bombay, 1895-98.

Aitareya Brahmana - Thomas Suprecht, Boun 1879.

Asvalayana Grhyahsutra - V.V.S. Ranade, Anandasran Sanskrit Series, Poona 1936.

Astadhyayi - Guru Prasad Shastri, Benaras 1951.

Apastamba Dharmasutra - Bombay Sanskrit Series, Bombay, 1932.

**Modern Work**

Acharya P.K. - Encyelopedia of Hindu Architecture Reprint, Delhi, 1974.

Ali Rahman - Art and Architecture of Kalacuries, Delhi; 1987.

- Art and architecture of Dasarna (Malwa) Region Delhi- 2008.

Andhare Shridhar - Chronology of Mewar Paintings, Delhi, 1987.

Awasthi R. - Khajuraho ki Deva Pratimayen (Hindi) Agra, 1967.

Agarwala R.A. - History, Art and Architecture of Jaisalmer, Delhi, 1979.

Agarwala - V.S. - Indian Art Varanasi, 1965.

Ambey Gann. - Cities of Mughal India.

Abul Fazl - Akbar Nama (tr.) N. Beyeridge 3 vol, Delhi, 1972-73.

- Ain-i-Akbari vol I (tr.) H. Beochman

- Calcutta 1873, Vol. II-III (tr.) H.S. Jerrett.

- Calcutta, 1891-92.

Barnes, Ernest - Dhar and Mandu, A. Guide, Bombay, 1902.

Brown Percy - Indian Architecture (Islamic period) Bombay, 1975)

Babur - Tuzuk-i-Baburi (Babar-nama) (te.) A.S. Beveridge, Delhi, 1970.

Begde P.V. - Ancient and Medieval Town Planning in India, Delhi, 1978.

Banerjee R.D. - Age of Emperial Gupta, Benaras, 1933.

Banerjee J.N. - Development of Hindu Iconography, Calcutta, 1941.

Bose N.S. - Development of Hindu Iconography, Calcutta, 1941.

# Index

## L



## M



## N



## O

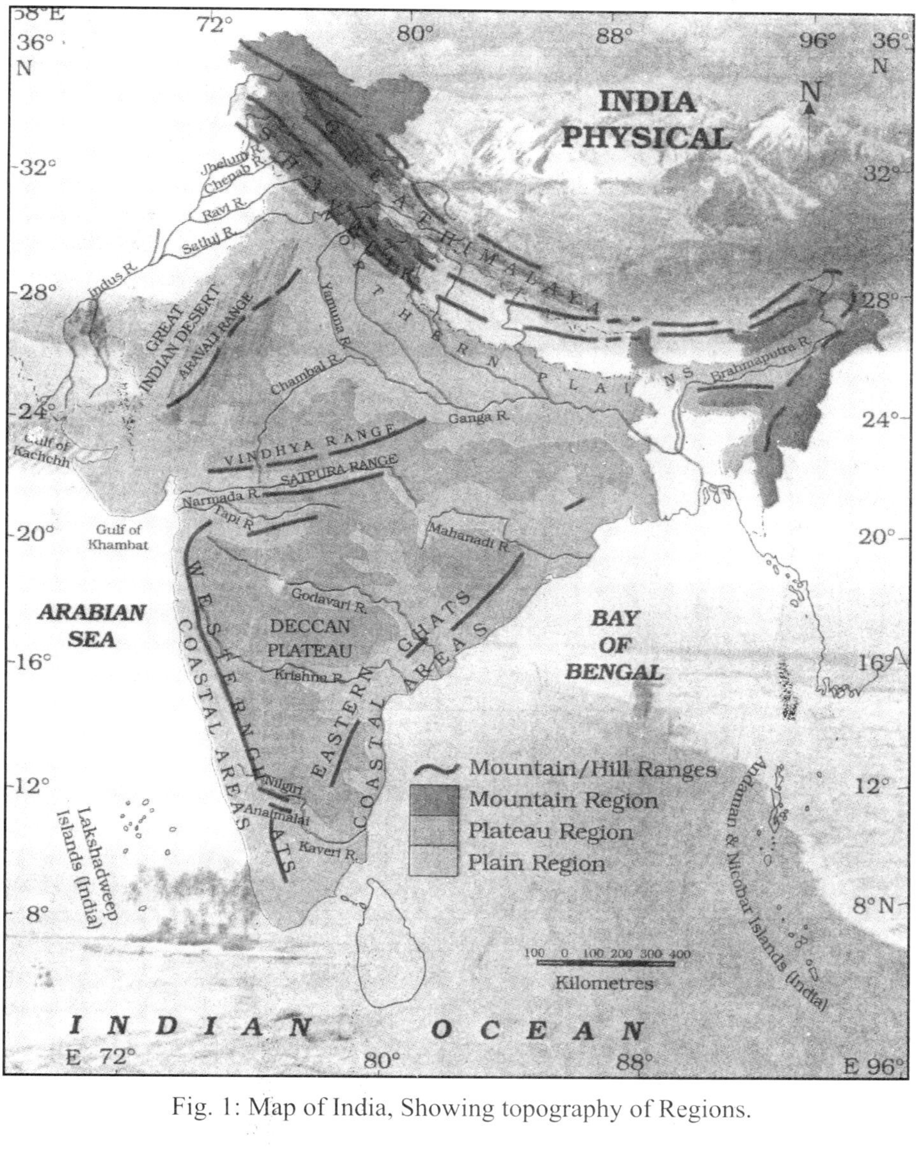


Fig. 1: Map of India, Showing topography of Regions.

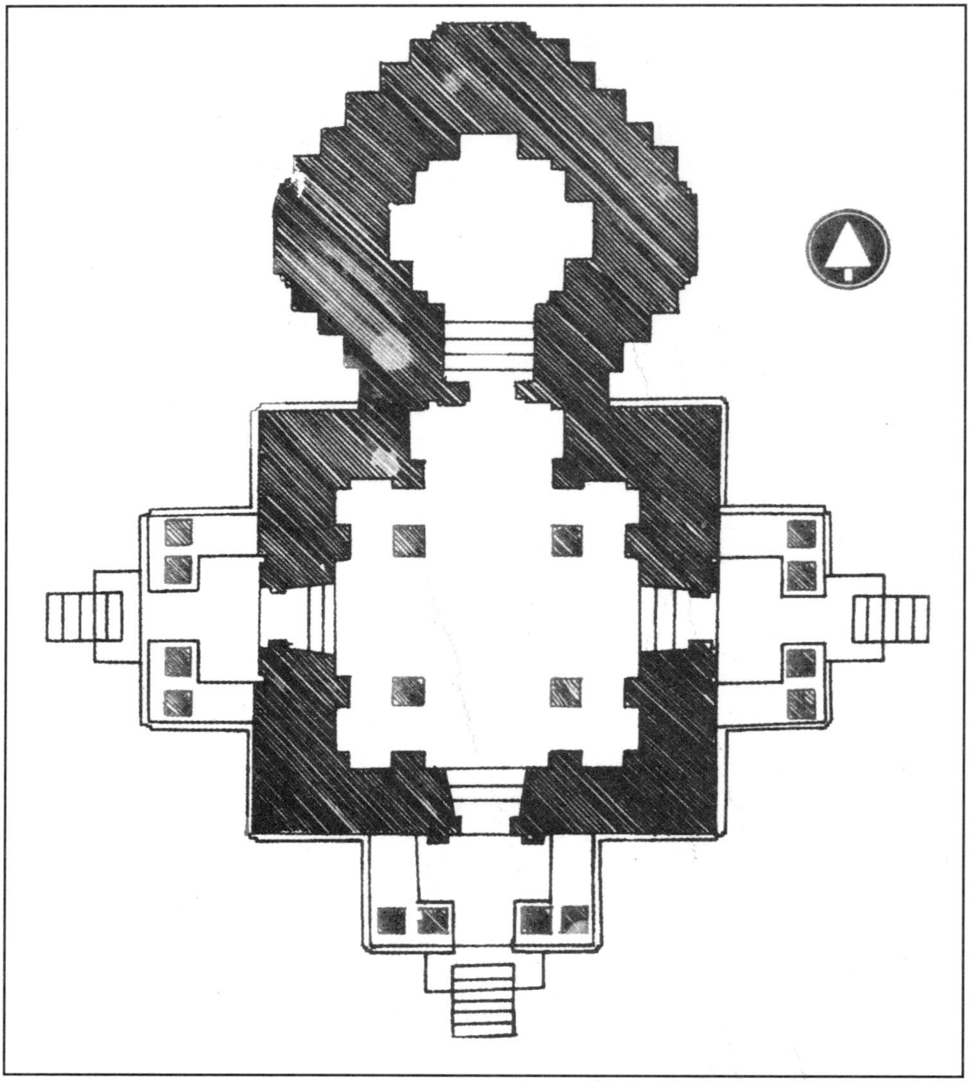

Fig. 2: Plan of Bhoramdeo temple (Chapari Distt. Kwardha)

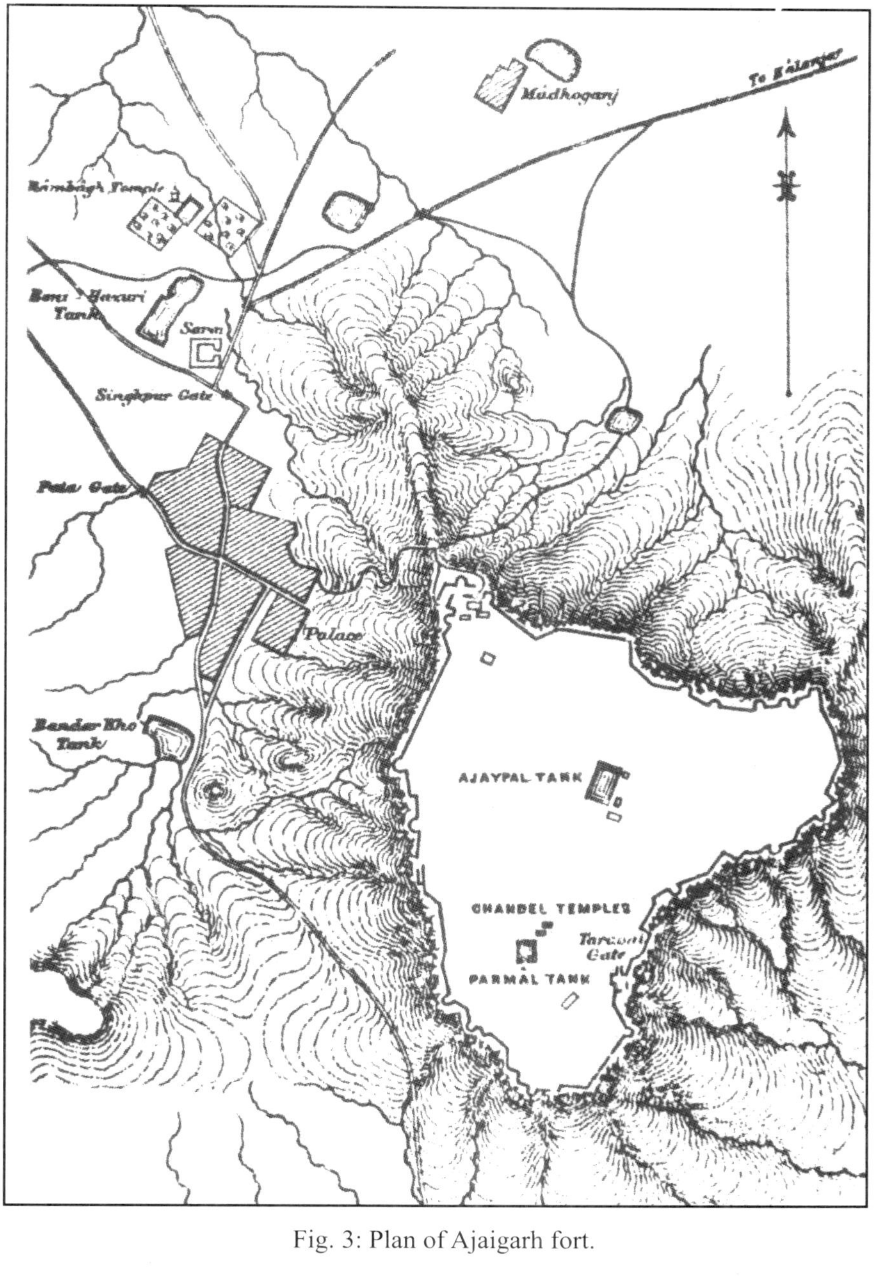


Fig. 3: Plan of Ajaigarh fort.

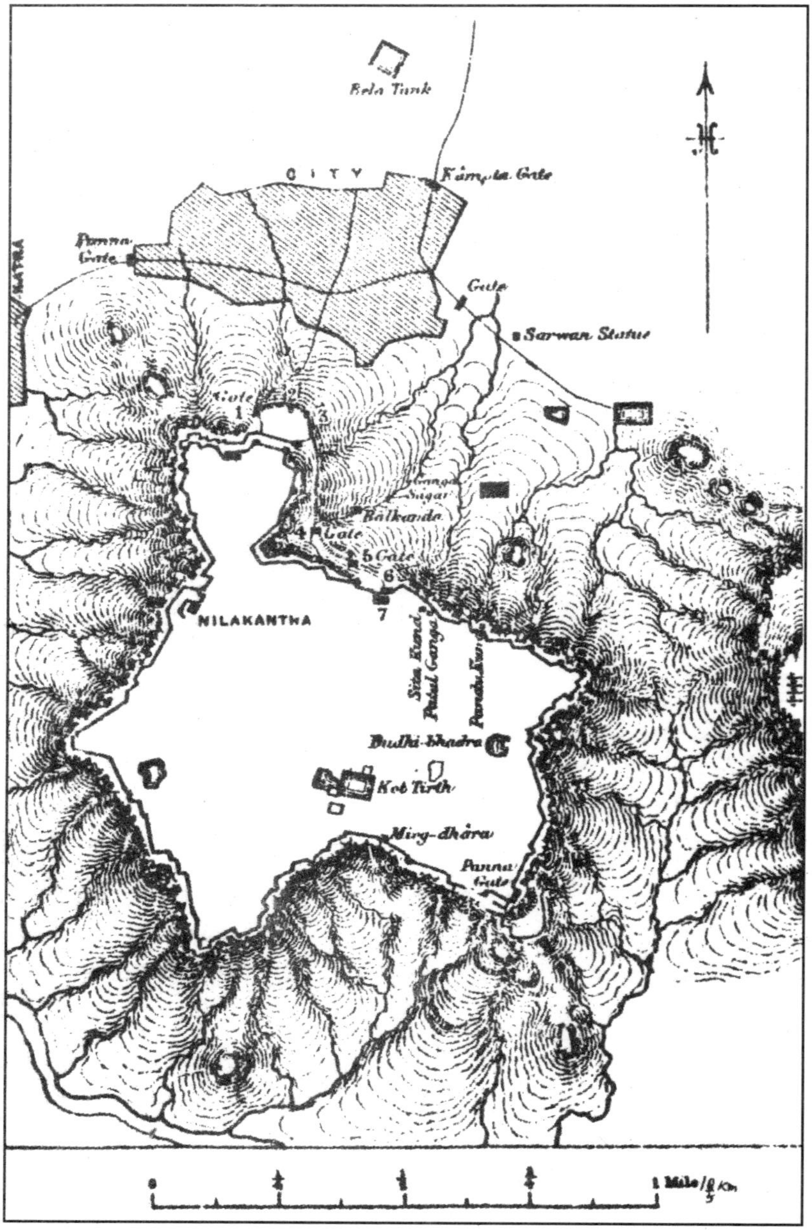


Fig. 4: Plan of Kalanjar fort.

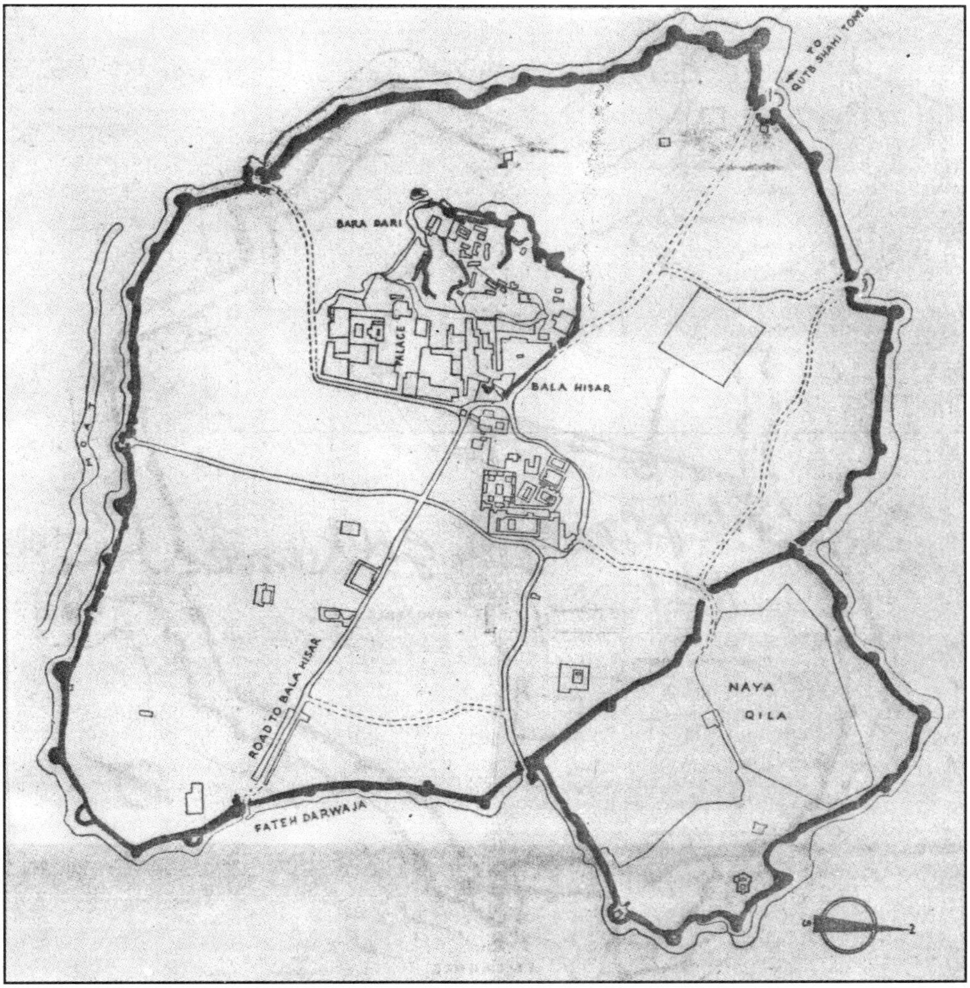


Fig. 5: Plan of Golkunda fort.

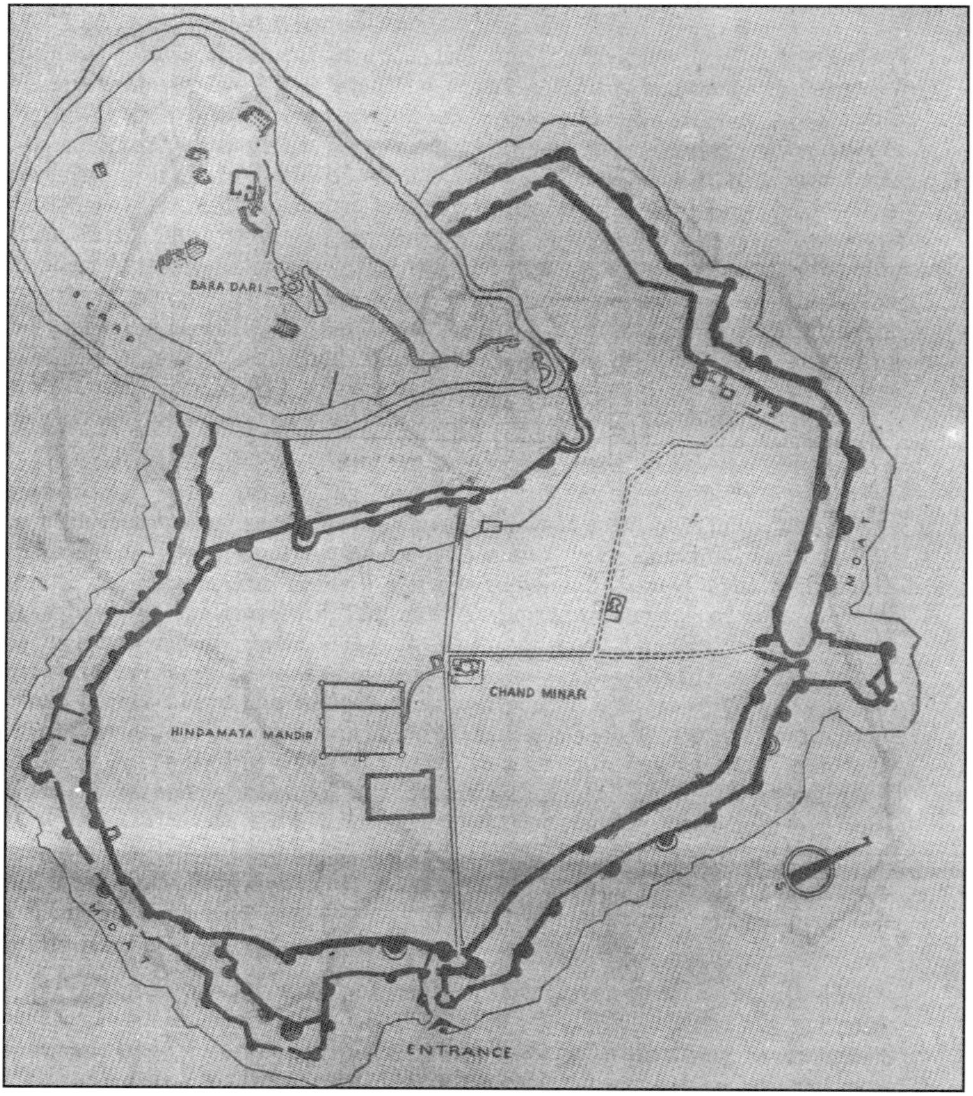


Fig. 6: Plan of Daultabad fort.

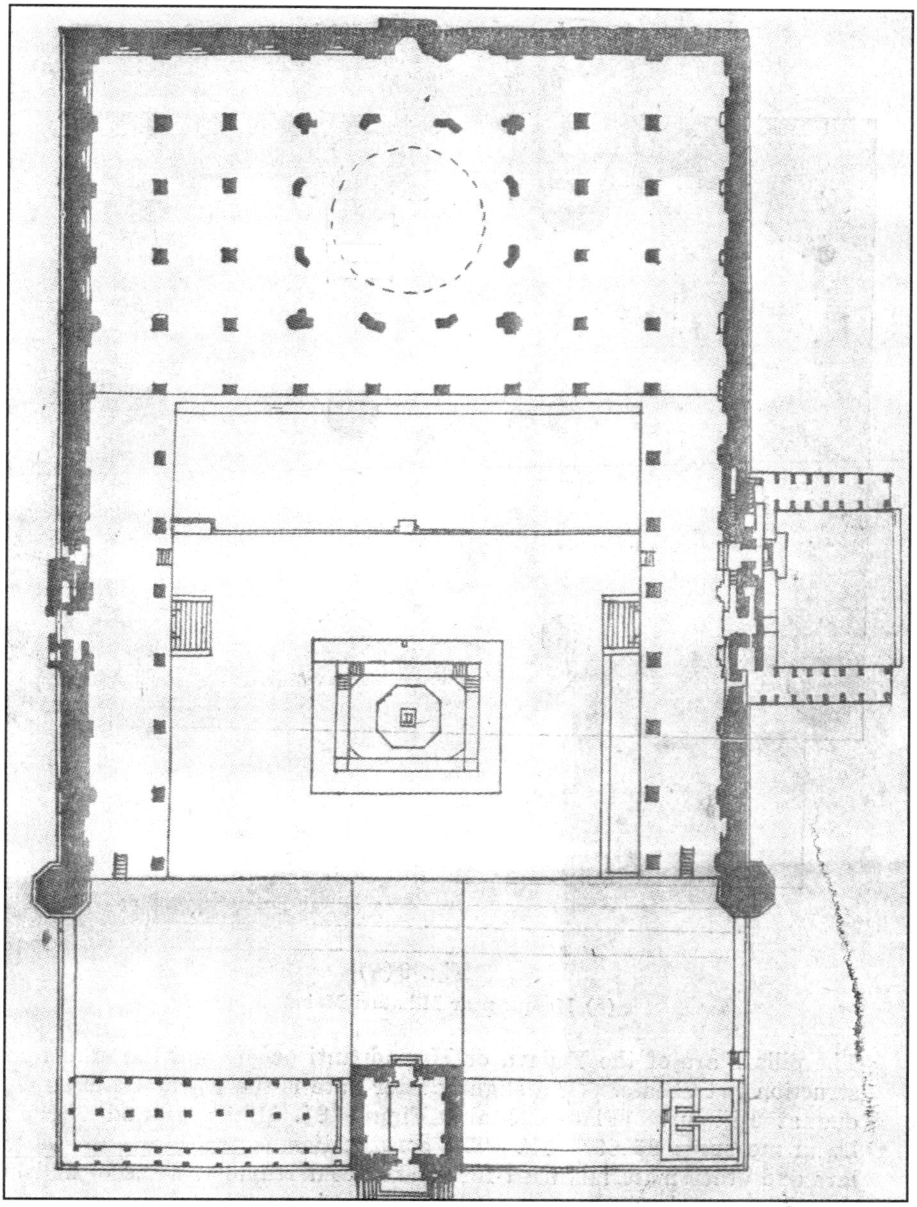

Fig. 7: Plan of Jami Masjid, Bijapur.

# PLATES

Pl. 1(A): Horse riding scene

Pl. 1(B): Hunting scene

Pl. 2: Seals from excavation at Mohan-Jodaro and Harappa, 3000 B.C. depiction of humped Bull. Harappan script and excavated structures

Pl. 3 (A): Steatite tablets depicting animal

Pl. 3 (B): Horned human figures

Pl. 4: Sanchi stupa I, general view depicting, Harmika, Chhaettreshti gateways, architraves

Pl. 5: Close up view of Sanchi Stupa I, Gateway, details of architraves

Pl. 6: Temple 17 Sanchi, Vidisha Gupta period 4th Century A.D.

Pl. 7: Ajanta Caves

Pl. 8: Mahabodhi Temple, Bodhgaya

Pl. 9: Bhojpur temple, after restoration

Pl. 10: Kandariya Mahadeo temple Khajuraho, Chhatarpur, (M.P.) Candella Period 10-11th Century A.D.

Pl. 11: Mother and Child Khajuraho, Chhatarpur (M.P.) Candella period 10-11th Century A.D.

Pl. 12: Udaiyshwar temple, Udaipur Vidisha

Pl. 13: A. General view of Gwalior Fort, Gwalior

Pl. 13: B. Teli ka Mandir, Gwalior Fort, Gwalior

Pl. 14: Man Mandir palace, Gwalior Fort, Gwalior

A

B

Pl. 15 (A&B): Shas-Bahu temple Gwalior Fort, Gwalior

Pl. 16: Delwara temple (Vimala Vashi) Mount Abu

Pl. 17: Ceiling of Vimal Vashi temple Mount Abu

Pl. 18: Mahakaleshwar temple, Ujjain

Pl. 19: Dwarkadhish temple, Gujarat

Pl. 20 (A): Chaturbhoj Temple at Orchha

Pl. 20 (B): Sun Temple, Osian

Pl. 21: Interior view of Jahangir Mahal, Orchha

Pl. 22: Raja Mahal, Orchha

Pl. 23: Bhoramdeo temple (Distt. Kwardha)

Pl. 24: Dhubela Mahal, Chatarpur (M.P.)

Pl. 25 : Qutb-Minar, Delhi

Pl. 26: Red Fort, Delhi, (intricate carvings)

Pl. 27: Humayun Makbara, Delhi

Pl. 28: Safdar Jang Tomb, Delhi

Pl. 29: Taj Mahal, Agra

Pl. 30: Lingraj Temple, Orissa

Pl. 31 (A): Sun Temple, Konark

Pl. 31 (B): Close up view of Wheel of Sun temple of Konark

Pl. 32: Shore Temple, Mahabalipuram

Pl. 33: Virupaksha Temple

Pl. 34: Kangra Fort, Himanchal Pradesh

Pl. 35: General View of Jaisalmer Fort, Rajasthan

Pl. 36: Keshava Temple, Somnathapur

Pl. 37: Gopuram, Vellore

Pl. 38 (A): General view of Golkunda Fort

Pl. 38 (B): General view of Asirgarh Fort, Burhanpur

Pl. 39: General View of Daultabad Fort, Daultabad

Pl. 40: Golgumbaj, Bijapur